The Smugglers' Banker

Banker

THE STORY OF ZEPHANIAH JOB
OF POLPERRO

Jeremy Rowett Johns

ISBN 978-0953001224
ISBN 0953001229

First edition published 1997
Second edition published 2008
Polperro Heritage Press,
Clifton-upon-Teme, Worcestershire WR6 6EN UK
www.polperropress.co.uk

Cover design by
Steve Bowgen

Printed by
4edge Limited
Hockley, Essex
United Kingdom

Contents

Illustrations

Fourth section

FOREWORD

It is doubtful that the true story of one of Cornwall's more remarkable citizens could have been written had not an eccentric amateur historian named Frank Hill Perrycoste arrived in the Cornish fishing village of Polperro around the year 1900.

Perrycoste quickly developed a keen interest in local history and offered to help Sir Francis Galton, the eminent scientist and pioneer of the study of fingerprints, by collecting the prints of the inhabitants of Polperro; Galton wanted to know if fingerprints were an inherited characteristic and could, therefore, be used to determine whether any two individuals were related. To chart the relationships of the men, women and children of Polperro he fingerprinted, Perrycoste also compiled pedigrees of the families who lived there.

Perrycoste's studies later led him to the archives of Talland and Lansallos, the two parishes that divide Polperro, and eventually to the accumulation of papers and ledgers left by Zephaniah Job the financier of smugglers and privateers nearly a century earlier. When Perrycoste came across the Job papers they were still stored in a worm-eaten chest at Crumplehorn Mill above Polperro and his account of the discovery relates how, after Job's death in 1822, 'certain malefactors made a huge bonfire' which destroyed a large quantity of the records.

Although many of the items that survived long enough for Frank Perrycoste to examine have since vanished, the substantial remainder is now in the Courtney Library at the Royal Cornwall Museum, Truro, and I am grateful to the Royal Institution of Cornwall for the kind assistance I have been granted there. In addition, I have received generous help from a number of people, in particular the author and historian James Derriman, the Polperro artist Sue Lord, and the Polperro Harbour Trustees who administer the Polperro Heritage Museum.

Publication of this book has been generously assisted by a grant from the Sir Arthur Quiller Couch Memorial Fund.

Jeremy Rowett Johns, 1996

INTRODUCTION

On a cold Spring afternoon in the year 1822, a group of villagers gathered round a blazing bonfire outside a lime-washed stone cottage above Polperro, one of the smallest and remotest fishing harbours on the south-east coast of Cornwall. From time to time someone would emerge from the doorway of the building clutching an armful of books and papers and throw them unceremoniously onto the crackling fire, pausing only briefly to watch as they curled in the heat and the flames began licking their scorched brown edges.

Every now and then the chill wind blowing down through the coombe behind the houses would gust, lifting a flurry of charred fragments high into the air where they hung for a moment before being carried out to sea.

A strange stillness enveloped the quayside that day. The bustle and noise that usually filled the area halted temporarily as if in deference to the man whose home the cottage had been; a man whose devotion to business and the community in which he lived had not only brought great prosperity during the years of goodness and plenty, but great comfort and support throughout the bad times.

Bonfires in Polperro traditionally marked events of special significance. Beacons had been lit on the cliffs nearby to warn smuggling vessels at sea it was unsafe to approach. Great fires had marked the end of the wars with France and the coming of peace. The communal bonfire of tar-barrels and faggots lit on the eve of the annual fair there in July was accompanied by singing and shouting as it burned. And now this fire, marking the end of an era, the end of another chapter in Polperro's remarkable history at the passing of one of its most respected adopted sons and citizens, Zephaniah Job.

Onto the bonfire went his ledgers, journals and account books, his cashbooks and the parchment bound letter-books that contained copies of correspondence relating to business dealings over decades with men and women from all walks of life. Many secrets perished in the flames as the circle of onlookers swelled, some curious, others content in the knowledge that their confidential financial affairs were at least safe from the prying eyes of those who had no business to know.

As dusk fell and a light drizzle began to fall, the flames flickered and died, leaving only a glowing heap of embers like the last remains of a funeral pyre. The crowd drifted away and an eerie emptiness filled the cottage whose contents had fuelled the flames.

Not everything of Zephaniah Job's was cremated that afternoon, however. Enough survived to tell the story of one of the most extraordinary Cornishmen ever. One hundred years later the curiosity of Frank Perrycoste,* another migrant to Polperro, led to the discovery of a residual horde of account books, ledgers and letter-books once belonging to Zephaniah Job that had lain decaying in the loft of Crumplehorn Mill above Polperro.

Perrycoste encountered more than half a hundredweight of material which had somehow escaped the flames in 1822. For the next twelve months he set about cataloguing, sifting and piecing together the enormous quantity of fragmented

---

* Frank Hill Perrycoste (1866-1929) developed a keen interest in local history after settling in Polperro with his wife at the end of the 19th century, offering to help Sir Francis Galton, the scientist and pioneer of the study of fingerprints, by collecting prints of Polperro inhabitants. Galton wanted to know if fingerprints could be used to determine whether any two individuals were related. To chart the relationships of the men, women and children whose fingerprints he obtained, Perrycoste also compiled pedigrees of the Polperro families concerned.

records that had fallen into his hands. And at the end of his labours, he published an account of his studies in 1930 entitled *Gleanings from the Records of Zephaniah Job of Polperro* in which he observed:

'This collection of records seems to me of very great value, as a huge quarry for social and economic data of various kinds and of both local and general interest during forty or fifty momentous years - a value that will necessarily increase as, with the progress of time, the past becomes more and more remote:'

Frank Perrycoste's *Gleanings* proved to be much more than just a revealing social study of 18th century life in Cornwall. They pieced together for the first time the many strands of a complex network of people and places involved in the clandestine trade of contraband goods of which Zephaniah Job had indeed been the central figure in Polperro.

1

Fugitive From St. Agnes

Zephaniah Job was born in the parish of St. Agnes, the centre of a large mining area on the north-west coast of Cornwall, sometime around the beginning of January, 1750. It was a time of great social and economic change marking the beginning of the Industrial Revolution that was to sweep through Cornwall during the latter half of the eighteenth century, bringing great wealth to a few and employment for many more.

The youngest of the five children of Zephanias and Sarah Job, Zephaniah was baptised at the Parish Church of St. Agnes on January 22nd 1750 by the Reverend James Walker, an event recorded in two separate volumes of the Parish Church Registers:

Zephania Son of Zephanias Job & Sarah his wife Bapt. 22 Jany 1749*

The same Registers record the baptism of Zephaniah's father in 1708 and his death in 1769. His mother, Sarah, gave birth to three sons and two daughters. Their first child, born in 1735 and baptised Zephanias, died in infancy. The second, John, was born a little over a year later, followed by a daughter Elisabeth in 1740 and another, Sarah, in 1744.

The family had moved to St. Agnes at the beginning of the eighteenth century from the parish of Gwithian to the west when Zephaniah's grandfather had come in search of work

---

* The baptism is shown as having taken place in 1749 because prior to 1752 two calendar systems were in use in England; the Civil or Legal year began on March 25th (Lady Day), while the Historical year began on January 1st.

among the flourishing mining industry there. St. Agnes is a large coastal parish whose main features are the St. Agnes Beacon, rising sharply inland to a height of over 600 feet and dominating the countryside to the west of the Trevaunance valley, and Trevaunance Cove which affords access by sea.

The Job family settled somewhere in the area between the sea and St. Agnes Beacon. One of the tenants recorded as having paid 5s 6d rent for a plot of land in nearby Goonfrey (Goonvrea today) at the time was a Zephany Job, in all probability the grandfather of Zephaniah.

The area around St. Agnes Beacon was rich in tin, copper and silver deposits and even in the mid-eighteenth century the landscape was scattered with mine-workings in every direction. Improvements in mining techniques and a growing demand for Cornish metals encouraged greater exploitation of such mineral deposits. This in turn gave employment to many thousands of people who otherwise had nothing other than subsistence farming or fishing to support themselves. By the time of Zephaniah Job's birth, a particularly rich vein of tin ore had just been discovered near St. Agnes at a site known as Polberro.

Cornish miners were a tough, hard-living race and the children of such mining communities were employed from an early age. Boys as young as eight years would be taught to sort the various ores, so getting to know them at a glance; at the age of 14 they would usually be sent underground. A few, those who displayed a quickness of learning and a natural ability to master complex techniques, would be singled out for special instruction. It is very likely that the young Zephaniah Job was marked out in this manner judging by the earliest reference to his childhood, in the *History of Polperro* published in 1871:

'[Job] received an education that was to fit him for the position of mine-captain, which requires, besides common arithmetic, a knowledge of mensuration and the lower branches of mathematics.'

While it may have been the ambition of many young men employed in the mines to become a mine captain,* only those who displayed exceptional qualities were likely to reach such a position. According to a 19th century issue of the *Mining Journal*:

'To fill this important office properly, the individual should be possessed of certain natural physical capabilities, one of the most important of which is a robust, sound constitution, as exposure to wet, and the fatigue of climbing the various pitches, backs and levels where the miners work, entail considerable bodily exertion. He should possess a quick eye, a retentive memory and a keen power of observation; these endowments should be improved and cultivated by a careful and suitable education, embracing more particularly the liberal sciences of mathematics, chemistry, geology, mineralogy, civil engineering, and a knowledge of accounts; in addition to all these, he should have extensive practical experience, so as to adapt them to his purposes.'

There is little doubt, as subsequent events were to demonstrate, that Zephaniah Job displayed many, if not all of these qualities and that, had he remained in St. Agnes to pursue his intended career in the mining industry there, he would indeed have fulfilled the expectations for him. But at some time around 1770 Job was involved in an incident that was to have a dramatic effect on the rest of his life. Years later, there was talk of his having killed another young man in a fight, but the only real clue to what happened is contained in the original draft manuscript of the *History of Polperro* where the author, Dr. Jonathan Couch (in later life, Job's physician and confidant), recalls:

---

* A mine captain was responsible for the direct management of the mine, ensuring that costs were tightly controlled as well as providing technical guidance to the adventurers under whose direction he was employed.

'[Job] had the misfortune in a fit of rage to beat a boy in such a manner that it was supposed his life was in danger.'

The published version refers only to Job as a 'very young man' being 'obliged to quit his home abruptly in consequence of some trouble he had brought upon himself in a fit of rage.'

Whatever the cause of his sudden outburst of temper and the assault that followed, the consequences were serious enough for Job to flee from his home in St. Agnes, leaving behind his family and every prospect of a promising career. There were rumours in later years that he had even killed another young man. The truth can only be guessed, but what is known is that the aspiring mine captain found himself a fugitive as a result with nowhere, apparently, to go.

Instinctively, perhaps, he set off eastwards across Cornwall with little more than the clothing he was wearing, aware that any other direction would soon bring him to the coast again. On foot, he would have had to cross the high moorland terrain that divides the rugged north coastline of Cornwall from the gentler undulating shoreline in the south, working his way steadily east and south for more than 30 miles until he had reached a point somewhere along the road between Fowey and Looe that led eventually to Plymouth. Here, fate again took a hand in leading him to his ultimate destination. Job turned off the road and made his way down to the sea, perhaps following one of the many ancient routes that led down through the thickly-wooded valleys that lay between the headlands that dominated that part of the coast. On, down, until he came to Polperro.

What compelled him to leave the road and make his way overland towards the seclusion of this small fishing village hidden from all but the sea? Whatever it was, it proved to be a turning point in the life of Zephaniah Job and the small, isolated community in which he was soon to find himself.

2

Polperro Schoolmaster

When Zephaniah Job came to Polperro on the south coast of Cornwall sometime around 1770, he could not have wished for a more secluded haven. Enclosed by the sea at the mouth of the narrow creek in which it lay, it was surrounded on the landward side by steep thickly-wooded slopes forming a natural barrier to the outside world. The arrival of a stranger in such a tightly-knit community would not have passed unremarked, though curiosity soon gave way to hospitality.

The cottages of the few hundred inhabitants crowded round the harbour in haphazard arrangement, some perched on rocky ledges, others back-to-back and side-to-side as if competing for space along the narrow, tortuous lanes that wound among them. Low roofs of slate and thatch rose up on either side while through the middle past the Green ran the fast-flowing torrent that divided the parish of Talland to the east from that of Lansallos in the west. Many of the houses belonging to the fishermen were constructed of ships' timbers and granite stone to withstand the storms that regularly swept up the Channel, and their occupants lived on the floor above the ground level cellars used for storing fish and other provisions for the winter months.

The stench of fish reeked everywhere on Polperro. It wafted in from the boats moored in the harbour and from the fish scales on the quay where the fishermen and jowters* with their slimy brown panniers bargained noisily with one another over the latest catch to be landed. It hung in the air and in the houses and clung to the clothing of all who came into contact with it.

* Jowters were travelling fish salesmen and women.

To a stranger such as Job, the smell would have seemed suffocatingly pungent at first. Only a year or so earlier when John Wesley had ridden into Polperro in 1768, the Methodist preacher recorded in his journal:

'The room over which we were to lodge being filled with pilchards and conger-eels, the perfume was too potent for me, so that I was not sorry when one of our friends invited me to lodge at her house.'

After preaching to a crowd of local inhabitants standing in torrential rain on the Green, Wesley accepted an offer to stay at the home of John Rommett in the Warren. Rommett was a fisherman and fish-curer and the odour of dried conger eel stored in the cellar beneath his living room soon persuaded the preacher to remain instead at Mrs Martin's house in Talland Lane.

To the people of Polperro, however, the smell represented their principal means of subsistence; and for many, their only livelihood. Generations of them had depended more on the sea than on the land for a meagre living despite the insecurity it afforded. The fishermen, like seafarers everywhere, were a hardy group of men resigned to a precarious existence dictated by the changing rhythm of the wind and the waves. While they were at sea, the women were employed salting, pressing, bulking and cleaning the fish ashore; and when they were not directly involved in this work women traditionally passed the time gathered in groups around the harbour knitting the distinctive knit-frocks worn by their menfolk.

Pilchards were an essential part of the Cornish economy, for much of the land above the cliffs was too poor to support much more than a few cottagers. In good years when the pilchard shoals arrived in abundance off the coast during the summer and autumn months, there was fish enough for all. But if the pilchards failed to arrive, or storms prevented the boats from putting to sea, everyone shared the hardship and hunger of a bleak winter ahead.

The fishermen themselves were ill-educated and most were illiterate, unable even to sign their own names. Their dialect, peculiar to that part of Cornwall, would certainly have been unfamiliar even to someone like Job from another part of the county. As soon as a boy was old enough to go to sea and earn his keep, some as young as eight years of age, any semblance of formal education gained at either of the two poorly managed charitable schools in Polperro at the time ended abruptly.

Education was the one thing the impoverished fugitive from St. Agnes had to offer in return for his keep. As a tutor to the children of the community into which he had come, Zephaniah Job very soon found he was able to provide himself with a modest income. One of his early pupils was a Polperro boy named John Clements whose arithmetic book was found among the documents salvaged by Frank Perrycoste. The home-made, hand sewn exercise book is filled with examples of multiplication of money, division, 'reduction' and something called *The Golden Rule or Rule of Three Direct*, all presented in Job's neat copperplate handwriting.

Clements was just seven years old when he sat down at Job's direction and learned the multiplication table that adorns the first page of the book, carefully inscribed with his name, *John Clements of Polperro*, above and the date below: *12th December 1775*. The arithmetical examples that follow, page after page, start simply enough but get progressively more difficult:

If one yard of Broadcloth cost 18s..7d what shall 5 pieces each piece 12 yards cost?

What shall 72 Ankers of Rum each 10 gallons cost at 4s..9d per gallon?

If 14s will buy 8lbs of Tobacco, how much will £14..8s buy at that rate?

Bought 42 Hundred[weight] of Tea at £10..15s..9d per Hundred. Sold it at 2s..3d per pound. What did I gain by the whole?

On a later page, recorded in the same neat copybook hand:

Division of Divers Denominations. This Rule sheweth you to equally divide almost any sum of money equally between different persons.

And on another, under the head of Reduction:

Reduction is of two kinds that is ascending and descending; descending is the bringing of a greater denomination into a lesser denomination as pounds into shillings, shillings into pence and this is performed by multiplication.

Such arithmetical axioms were widely taught in schools in the eighteenth century and Job's pupils were probably required to recite them from memory as well as use them to solve the sort of baffling exercises illustrated in Clements' book:

How many barleycorns will reach round the globe it being accounted 360 degrees, each degree 60 miles?

The answer given is a mind-boggling total of 4105728000 barleycorns, although modern mathematical students would not even be expected to know that a barleycorn was a measure of length in common use at the time equal to one third of an inch. Another exercise requires the number of seconds in 38 solar years to be calculated; and another even the number of wagons that would stretch end to end from Fowey to Looe 'allowing six yards for the standing of each waggon', though no clue is given as to the distance between the two towns..

Such exercises are an indication of the flair and fascination for figures that Job demonstrated throughout his life. They also provide an illuminating insight into the cost of living in Polperro at the time: a man's yearly income is given as £29..18s..9d; a sheep could be bought for 12s..9d, while brandy was 7s..6d a gallon, rum 4s..9d a gallon and tea 2s..3d a pound, though from whom such goods could be purchased at these prices is not revealed. John Clements' little book does reveal, however, the extent to which Job adapted his instruction according to the needs of the families whose children he taught. Calculations almost always involved quantities of tea, tobacco, brandy and rum, all commodities then passing through Polperro as contraband.

When John Clements was older he went to sea and eventually became captain of the schooner *Polperro* trading between Cornwall and Ireland. Job became a part owner of the vessel and, wasting nothing, he later used the blank pages at the back of the school book he had prepared for his young pupil in 1775 to record the schooner's accounts between 1787 and 1808.

Job's attempt to establish a school of his own was not a great success however. In a community where the ability to earn a livelihood depended more on the skills of seamanship than scholarship, there was little regard for the need for children to be taught how to read and write. To supplement the meagre income he earned from teaching, Job soon found he could help the Polperro boatowners in other ways; as book-keeper, general correspondent and advisor for their business affairs, relieving them of hours of tedious paperwork.

The boats were invariably owned by syndicates, small groups of fishermen and others who would take a share in the cost of buying and fitting out a vessel. Venturers were also encouraged to take shares in a voyage in the hope of profiting upon the boat's safe return. Whatever learning the fishermen lacked was more than compensated for by their seamanship, courage and natural shrewdness when facing the elements at sea. And if there were no fish to be had, there was a harvest of an altogether different kind awaiting those bold enough to gather it.

Generations of Polperro mariners had supplemented their living by bringing contraband ashore, often at secluded coves along the coast near Polperro under cover of darkness. In nearby Lantivet Bay, boats would land stealthily in Palace Cove or Parsons Cove and the goods carried up the narrow sunken lane that still leads today to Lansallos church. Others came into Talland Bay where, once landed on the beach, the illicit cargoes would quickly disappear into the churchyard above or be taken away inland along well-trodden paths to secret hiding-places where they could be stored safely before being distributed.

Sheer economic necessity drove the Polperro seafarers to smuggling. In Cornwall it increased steadily throughout the eighteenth century to such an extent that it became a major activity there. Successive British governments had imposed high duties on a variety of luxury goods imported from Europe, initially to protect trade with the North American colonies, and smuggling became exceptionally profitable for anyone prepared to face little more risk than most people encountered in their everyday struggle to earn a livelihood. Understaffed revenue authorities were invariably powerless to prevent the smugglers, who were often protected by a sympathetic public.

Brandy, gin, tea and tobacco were all readily available across the Channel at considerably lower prices than they were in England where such commodities attracted heavy duties and were often unobtainable. By 1770 some 469,000 gallons of brandy and 350,000 pounds of tea alone were being smuggled into Cornwall every year amounting to the considerable loss of some £150,000 to the Exchequer.

Because the Channel Islands were exempt from any taxation imposed by a British parliament they become the main centre for the supply of contraband goods into Britain during the 17th and 18th centuries. The Guernsey merchants at St. Peter Port imported large quantities of geneva (gin) from Rotterdam, brandy from France and Spain, rum from the West Indies, tobacco from Virginia and tea via the powerful East India Company from China. Most of these commodities were sold on to English wholesalers and smugglers.

Cornwall's proximity to Guernsey ensured such trade was particularly active there, but the 100 miles of sea separating Polperro from St. Peter Port involved a hazardous voyage for small fishing vessels in all but the most favourable weather, even in times of peace. With only the crudest of navigational instruments to guide them, the men who made the perilous crossing often risked death at sea and many were lost in the attempt to bring back contraband goods.

When the tax on salt was increased by the young William Pitt in order to raise money to pay for the wars against France, Cornish pilchard fishing communities were particularly hard hit. Large quantities of salt were used in preserving pilchards for markets both at home and abroad, and the extra tax burden only served to encourage an illegitimate trade with Britain's enemy, France, from which country much salt was normally obtained.

For ordinary folk, the only way to get cheap salt to cure enough fish for their own families was by smuggling it into the country. It required a bushel of salt to cure a thousand pilchards, barely enough to supply a moderately large family throughout the winter, but the duty on such a quantity of English salt, amounting to 3s. 4d (6s. 8d for foreign salt), represented nearly half the wages made in a poor fishing season.

Britain's restrictive trading laws and high taxes also led to her North American colonies making their historic Declaration of Independence in 1776. When war broke out between Britain and the rebel colonists, France and Spain joined the rebels in order to gain revenge on Britain for territorial and trade losses suffered in earlier years.

A few weeks after France had declared war on Britain in February 1778, a letter arrived at the home of Zephaniah Job in Polperro that was to implicate the erstwhile schoolmaster in the contraband trade carried on there for many years to come.

3

Freetraders and Privateers

The letter arrived in Polperro aboard one of the smuggling vessels addressed to *Z Joab at Poolparrow*, dated February 20th 1778 and signed Jean Guille Junior & Co. The Guilles were Guernsey merchants whose business at St. Peter Port had prospered from the trade in spirits and other goods with dealers along the coast of England. Job had evidently already indicated his willingness to act as the Guilles' agent since the letter acknowledged his agreement to do so, offering the usual commission on all money received and enclosing a number of outstanding accounts for the same Cornish smugglers who had recommended him:

'Mr John Baker* recommended you to us and we make no doubt you will be punctual in executing every order we commit to your care. You are, we suppose, acquainted with the commission for your trouble in receiving and remitting which is ½ per cent besides all other charges such as postage and expences in riding out if it so occurs, which last you will do with as much economy as possible.'

Like other Guernsey merchants, Jean Guille & Co. preferred to deal through an agent such as Job rather than directly with the smugglers in order to ensure the goods supplied were paid for. For his part, Job knew very well that such business was illegal. He would have been aware that much of the brandy, rum and geneva sold in the neighbourhood

---

* John Baker was an active member of the Polperro smuggling fraternity who also made a substantial profit from privateering ventures, including the *Swallow* [see Chapter 4].

had been brought ashore illicitly, often under the nose of the resident Custom House officer in Polperro, Thomas Pinsent But he knew too that the trade was vital to the livelihood of the families that lived there.

Soon Job was also acting as the agent for other Guernsey merchants, including Messrs Jersey & De Lisle and Peter Mourant the numerous entries in his day-book for 1778 reveal the extent of his dealings with the Polperro smugglers. In March alone he collected over £700 in payments from them for goods obtained in St. Peter Port, money which he forwarded in turn, through a London agent, to the suppliers.

The goods were shipped aboard the Polperro boats to order and the smugglers allowed several months credit for each cargo. Most of the Polperro vessels were fast sailing luggers, shallow draft boats able to operate in strong tidal currents and rocky shores. Built for speed and manoeuvrability, they were manned by men who had been born to the sea with an intimate local knowledge of the tides and currents. When venturing across the Channel or on longer cruises they often carried a large crew capable of handling the sails and out-running even the deep-keeled Revenue cutters patrolling offshore.

Whenever war broke out between Britain and one of her foes in the latter half of the 18th century, there were plenty of people anxious to profit from the hostilities that ensued. Among the first to take advantage were the privateers, privately owned armed vessels granted special authorisation by the Admiralty to attack and seize enemy shipping. Many vessels previously engaged in smuggling were fitted out as privateers in Guernsey. And when France joined the war on the side of the American rebels in 1778, there was a rush of applications from Channel Island and Cornish boat owners for the necessary licences to cruise in search of enemy vessels.

Privateering involved a great deal of clerical and administrative work. Letters of marque* authorising the

* A letter of marque was a commission issued on behalf of the sovereign licensing the commander of a privately owned ship to cruise against enemy vessels in time of war.

seizure of enemy shipping had to be obtained from the Admiralty, requiring the vessel's commander or someone acting on his behalf to attend a hearing in London. Money had to be raised to fit out the vessels concerned; stores and weapons purchased and accounted for before putting to sea. And when a prize was captured, it had to be legally condemned in a prize court - a complex and expensive process that required the appointment of an agent to deal with. All this involved hours of laborious paperwork and book-keeping. From his confined living quarters in Polperro, Job conducted most of his business by correspondence with agents, lawyers, bankers and merchants in London, Guernsey and elsewhere.

In Polperro, the renewed hostilities with France in 1778 created a flurry of activity around the harbour as owners and venturers alike hurried to take advantage of the situation. Job was besieged by fishermen and boatowners seeking his help in preparing their vessels for sea as privateers in the hope of capturing lucrative French and American prizes. As with smuggling, the risks were great but the rewards were even greater still.

Job's first involvement with privateering concerned a vessel called the *Swallow* and was soon to meet with quite spectacular success. The *Swallow*, a fine three-masted lugger armed with 16 guns and carrying a crew of up to 50 men, was originally owned and fitted out as a privateer in Guernsey where she seized several French merchant ships carrying provisions for the rebel colonists in North America in the weeks immediately following France's entry into the war. Within a couple of years, however, Job and four other Polperro venturers had bought the *Swallow* and spent more than £1,500 refitting and arming her before putting to sea again in the summer of 1781. During the next two years, the *Swallow* was to capture no less than half a dozen valuable Franch prizes, the proceeds of which provided the basis for Job's subsequent business activities.

When Holland and Spain joined the hostilities in 1780, opportunity for the Polperro privateers to prey upon foreign merchant shipping passing through the Channel increased still further. Job was kept busy applying for letters of marque against Dutch craft; each application he made to the Admiralty Court required the name of the vessel concerned, its tonnage, crew size, armaments (including small arms and cutlasses), how long it was provisioned for and the names of the commander, officers and principal owners.

His application on behalf of the *Swallow*, for example, recorded that the vessel had a cargo carrying capacity of 80 tons and described it as having a square stern, three masts and was mounted with 16 carriage guns. It was also equipped with 40 small arms, 40 cutlasses, 20 barrels of gunpowder, 30 rounds of large shot and about one hundredweight of small shot, two sets of sails, three anchors and four cables. The *Swallow*'s crew numbered 50, of whom a third were landsmen, and the ship was victualled for six months. As well as himself, Job gave the names of four Polperro men as her principal owners: John Quiller,* William Johns, David Thompson and Richard Pascoe.

Another Polperro privateer whose accounts Job kept at the time was the *Good Intent*. Built at the nearby Polruan shipyard, it was a larger version of the *Swallow*, equipped with 28 guns and carrying a crew of 70 - enough to provide a prize crew in the event of success at sea. Following the capture of the *Snell Jager*, Job listed the names of 64 crewmen on board the *Good Intent* at the time, including her commander Sharrock Jenkins and master Charles Polgrain, adding a note that the *Snell Jager*, sailing from Cadiz to Ostend, had been taken in partnership with another vessel called the *Garland* from Plymouth.

Within a year or so, however, the intensive scale of attacks by British privateers and naval vessels on enemy shipping forced the withdrawal of much of the Dutch mercantile fleet. And when peace came again at the beginning of 1783 the Polperro luggers that had been hastily fitted out as privateers returned to port and the smuggling trade with Guernsey flourished once more.

---

* John Quiller (1741-1804) [see Chapter 6].

The Customs authorities were well aware of the dual purpose to which such vessels were often put, both in times of peace and war. From time to time warnings would be issued to their officers, as in May 1794:

'Information having been received by the Board that the smugglers have adopted a plan of building luggers and long open shallops* of sixty feet keel and upwards, and that it is the practice for them to obtain Letters of Marque for the former under sanction of fitting them out as privateers, and licences for the latter as boats to carry mackerel. That when the same are registered and completely fitted, they sail directly for Guernsey where the said vessels are sold to other owners, and immediately employed in the smuggling trade.'

These were the years in which small Cornish shipyards at Fowey and Mevagissey were busy turning out sloops and luggers in large numbers. In 1797 Job leased the cove under Peak Rock at the entrance to Polperro harbour to a boat-builder named James Henna to build a shipwright's yard.** The luggers built there were fine seaworthy vessels ranging from 20 tons to as big as 100 tons and their simple fore and aft rig made them ideal for coasting, as certain individuals in Guernsey knew well when they bought them for smuggling.

During the French wars many were converted into privateers and launched complete with twelve to sixteen gun-ports and deck stanchions. The sail area was often increased by fitting a longer bowsprit in order to give the extra turn of speed necessary for privateering. This was all very well as long as the vessel was engaged in legitimate cruising against the enemy, but if and when she indulged in a little smuggling and was chased, she could easily outstrip the slower Revenue

---

* Shallops were small, light fishing vessels of about 125 tons, usually rigged with lug sails.
** James Henna was subsequently committed to Exeter Asylum in 1805 at the age of 35 where he remained until at least 1817. The cost of his board, at 15 shillings a week, and other expenses met by the parish of Lansallos were paid by Job.

cutter. Hence the official precautions taken to ensure that such luggers should, unless actually in commission as privateers, be fitted with shorter 'legal' bowsprits,

It was not unusual for these vessels to be impounded, as in March 1791 when the Customs Board in London informed the Plymouth officials:

'A vessel between 60 and 70 feet long, lately built at Mevagissey for the smuggling employ, and owned by John Quiller of Polperro, has sailed from Mevagissey without being registered. She was then rigged as a sloop, but it is supposed she has since altered into a lugger...'

A month later the Customs Board wrote again:

'Having read your reports in return to our enquiry on the petition of John Quiller praying the delivery of a vessel called the Betsy under seizure at your port, on account of the bowsprit exceeding the dimensions prescribed by law, we have rejected his request and direct you to prosecute the vessel in the Exchequer.'

The *Betsy* would have suffered the usual fate of vessels condemned under the increasingly stringent anti-smuggling laws and, unless taken into service by the revenue service, have been sawn through in three places to ensure that she would never put to sea again. Regulations were introduced affecting the construction, equipment and crewing of sailing craft. Any vessel of more than 50 tons rigged as a lugger or having a bowsprit more than two-thirds its own length was liable to forfeiture. The law struck at everything concerned with smuggling. Boats, horses and carts used in the landing or transporting of contraband goods were seized and sold. The mere fact of loitering near the coast was sufficient to bring someone, however innocent their intentions, within the law's grasp:

'Any person loitering within five miles of the sea-coast

or any navigable river, with intent, as is suspected, to assist in running goods, is to be brought before a justice; and if unable to give a satisfactory account of his calling or employment, shall be committed to the House of Correction, to be whipped and kept to hard labour for any time not exceeding one month.'

The threat of such harsh penalties did little to deter the Polperro smugglers, however. When the young William Pitt reduced some of the heaviest duties on imports soon after he became Prime Minister in 1784 in the hope of discouraging the activities of smugglers, the trade between Guernsey and Cornwall continued unabated.

4

The *Swallow's* Tale

No vessel occupied more of Zephaniah Job's time than the *Swallow*. More than a dozen pages of his ledger covering the period between 1778 and 1786 were devoted to the *Swallow's* accounts from early in 1781 when the lugger was refitted by her new owners at Polperro before setting out in July under the command of Thomas Effard for Portugal. Job had already become one of the *Swallow's* owners and he arranged with one of the Lisbon merchants, probably Messrs John O'Neill, for her to take on a cargo of best Bohea tea, port wine and other goods that would make a handsome profit for her owners and 22 crewmen on their return. Since it was not unusual for such cruises to combine privateering with a little smuggling enterprise, her crew would have been hopeful of bringing a valuable prize home as well.

Their chance came a few days later off the north west coast of Spain. After crossing the Bay of Biscay where the *Swallow* encountered gale force winds and heavy seas, they caught sight of a storm-damaged vessel under jury rig making for the Spanish port of Corunna. Giving chase, the *Swallow's* crew soon saw that it was a French merchantman, *La Rusee*, whose mainmast had been carried away in the storm. As darkness fell, the *Swallow* closed on its stricken quarry and for over an hour the two vessels attempted to outmanoeuvre one another, exchanging sporadic gunfire as the *Rusee* tried desperately to fend off its smaller foe. Only after several broadsides from the *Swallow's* guns had torn into his already shattered rigging did the captain of the *Rusee*, Alexander Louvrier, realised the hopelessness of his situation and gave the order to strike colours and surrender.

A boarding party from the *Swallow* found the *Rusee* laden with military stores, tea, bales of cloth, silks and other goods intended for the rebel colonists in North America. Aware that he had captured a valuable cargo as well as a crew that outnumbered his own the *Swallow*'s commander, Thomas Effard, decided to return at once to Plymouth with the prize, having put nearly half his own crew aboard her.

Much to his dismay, however, they were joined two days later by a large 18-gun Liverpool privateer, the *Harlequin*, whose captain Joseph Fayrer offered to escort the *Swallow* and her prize to a British port in return for a twenty per cent share of the prize money. With barely enough men to crew both vessels and guard 35 prisoners, the *Harlequin*'s offer of 'protection' was one that Effard was hardly in a position to refuse, whatever he might think of one British privateer grabbing a share of the spoils of war of another. His fears were confirmed when, after four days in convoy together, he received a signal to bring the *Swallow* alongside the *Harlequin* who promptly ran out her guns when he did so. Effard was ordered by Captain Fayrer to bring his ship's papers aboard the *Harlequin* at once or he would give the order to open fire.

Seizing Effard's papers, including the *Swallow*'s commission to seize French vessels, Fayrer claimed they were invalid because the *Swallow* was a smuggler and confined Effard under armed guard below for an hour while he considered his next move. With a rich French prize in his possession and only the word of a band of Cornish smugglers to gainsay him, Fayrer decided to take advantage of the situation. Returning the *Swallow*'s commander to his own vessel with a party of men from the *Harlequin*, he ordered the Polperro crew and their prisoners aboard the Liverpool privateer and headed for Cork on the southern coast of Ireland in the hope of gaining legal possession of the captured prize.

Fayrer left the *Rusee* in the hands of a small prize crew from the *Harlequin* at Cork, a busy maritime city whose large harbour teemed with naval and mercantile ships of all sizes and nationalities, pending the outcome of the inevitable claims to her as a prize of war. Meanwhile, he escorted the *Swallow* to Liverpool where the *Harlequin*'s agent instituted a claim for a share of the prize money due from the capture of the *Rusee*.

News of the *Swallow*'s seizure reached Polperro within a matter of days of her arrival at Liverpool at the end of July, causing great concern to the families of the crew as well as to Zephaniah Job and the other owners. Job set off at once for Liverpool, taking with him sufficient cash for Thomas Effard and the rest of the crew. On arrival, he at once appointed an agent to procure the vessel's release before travelling on by land and sea to Cork.

Job spent the next three months in Cork where he sought condemnation of the *Rusee* as a legal prize of war. Admiralty Court procedure required three or four members of the prize vessel's crew, including the master, to answer a series of standard questions designed to establish the nationality, destination and ownership of the arrested vessel and its cargo, as well as the circumstances of its capture. Job engaged the services of a local notary, Thomas Chatterton, to act as the *Swallow*'s agent at the lengthy court hearings in the Town Hall at Cork. These continued until the end of October, with the testimony of those members of the *Rusee*'s crew who gave evidence having to be laboriously translated by an interpreter. The story of the capture of the *Rusee* and the subsequent encounter with the *Harlequin* was recounted in great detail, as were the contents of the French vessel's cargo: bales of cloth, various military stores and surgical instruments, tea, brandy, salt, as well as a large consignment of ladies' shoes, silks and other fashion accessories intended for the American market.

When, finally, judgement was given in favour of the *Swallow*, Job sailed with the *Rusee* from Cork round to the Port of London where he spent several more weeks disposing of both the vessel and her cargo, yielding a total of nearly £9,000 for her new owners. He gave instructions to William De Jersey, one of the several London agents with whom he dealt on behalf of the Polperro privateers, to invest the proceeds. But before Job received his share, De Jersey died suddenly in

Frank Hill Perrycoste (c1900)

Zephaniah Job's ledgers and letter-books
(courtesy of the Courtney Library, RIC)

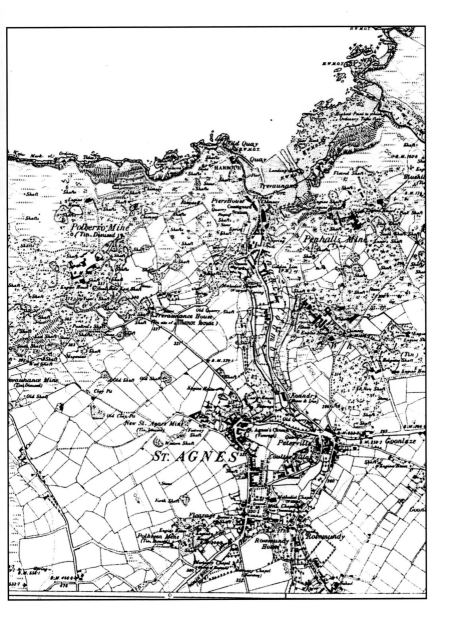

St. Agnes and district (OS 1888)

South view of Polperro (1813)
(by Joseph Farrington RA)

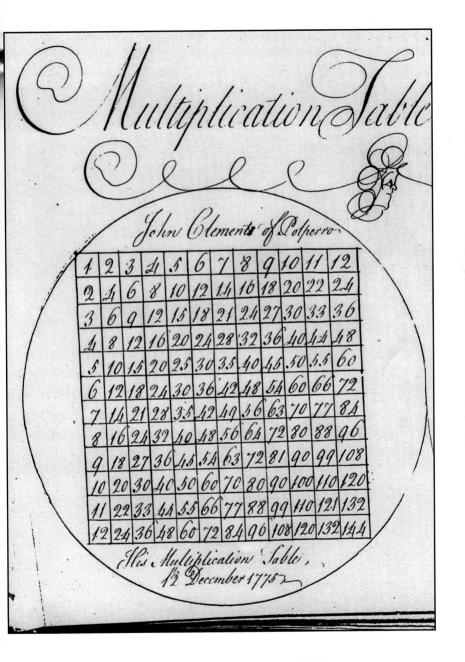

John Clements' exercise book (1775)
(Royal Institution of Cornwall)

To Joab. at Poolsparrow

We Send you the following

£ 44 "5:0. —— on John Rowett of the
44 " 5:0 —— on John Baker — of d:
44 " 5:0 —— on Reginald Barrett of d
44 " 5 · 0 — on Will: Longmaid of d
44 " 5 · 0 — on Charles Polgreen of
50 " 0 " 0 — on Tho: Bartlett — of d
12 " 15 " 0 — on Jacob Borlase — of d

£ 284 " 0 · 0 — together Two hundred Eighty
accepted and when paid please to remit
Jersey in London on our Acco:t. Mr John
us and we make no doubt you will be
Order we com't to your care; You are
Commission for your trouble in receive
besides all other charges Such as postage
Occurs which last you will do with as
We write Mr Tho: Bartlett to pay
pursuant the above Bill of which we
as well as to Mr Jacob Borlase of St
Seal the Letters after you have seen them

Jean Guille letter to Job, February 1778
(Priaulx Library, Guernsey)

FOR SALE, at the New Inn, in Polperro, on Monday the 3d day of March, 1783, at two o'clock in the afternoon,

The Good Polacre SAN LUIS DE BILBOA; Round sterned; burthen 120 tons, more or less, and is on account of her easy draught of water, swift sailing, and excellent order and condition, a very desirable vessel; her cables, sails, and rigging, are almost new; and being well found, may be sent to sea immediately, at little or no expence; now lying in the harbour at Fowey, and there to be delivered.

Immediately after the Sale of the San Luis de Bilboa, will be exposed to Sale,

The Good Chasemaree SAGE ALEXIS; Round sterned; burthen 50 tons, more or less; supposed to be two years old; is a remarkable strong built vessel, with her masts, yards, sails, cables, anchors, standing and running rigging, as she came from sea; now lying at Polperro, and there to be delivered.

Immediately after the Sale of the Sage Alexis will be Sold,

The Good Chasemaree ST ANNE D'ARSON; Round sterned; burthen 30 tons, more or less; her masts, yards, sails, cables, anchors, standing and running rigging, were new with the vessel about nine months since; and is as complete a vessel of her burthen as any in England; now lying also at Polperro, and there to be delivered.

Immediately after the Sale of the St. Anne D'Arson will be Sold,

The Good Schooner LE CHARDON; Round sterned; burthen 30 tons, more or less; being lately fitted out by the French for a privateer, has all her materials and sails in excellent good order; now lying in the harbour at Polperro, and there to be delivered.

Immediately after the Sale of the Le Chardon will be Sold,

About 38 Tons of FRENCH YELLOW ROSIN, Of exceeding good quality, which will be put up in lots for the convenience of the purchasers.

N. B. The above vessels were taken from the French and Spaniards by the Swallow private ship of war, John Quiller, Commander.

Samples of the rosin, and inventories ~~of the vessels~~, may be had, and the vessels seen, by applying to Zephaniah Job, in Polperro.

Polperro, February 18, 1783.

Job's Sale Notice
Sherborne & Yeovil Mercury, 1783

South East view of Trelawne (1815)
(engraving by C. S. Gilbert)

Trelawne (c1860)
(photograph by Lewis Harding)

November 1784 and his affairs were left in the care of his son-in-law, Thomas Bowerbank.

Bowerbank at first disputed Job's claim to the proceeds of the *Rusee*'s sale, then delayed payment of the money due to the *Swallow* owners for several years. Job pursued the matter in a series of increasingly impatient letters to Bowerbank, the last in August 1788 which ended: 'you will in the end pay dear for the unwarrantable delays you have occasioned.' Frustrated by Bowerbank's refusal to settle the matter, Job asked his legal advisor, Charles Rashleigh of St. Austle, to sue for recovery of the debt. At long last, eight years after the *Rusee* had been seized by the *Swallow*, Job received the sum of more than £500 due to him from the proceeds.

While the protracted legal and financial matters resulting from the *Swallow*'s capture of the *Rusee* were being resolved, the *Swallow* continued to earn substantial prize money for her owners from her privateering exploits.

A little over a year after the *Rusee* incident, in September 1782, Thomas Effard was again in command of the *Swallow* when she captured the French privateer schooner *Le Chardon* off Lands End without a shot being fired. In December under the command of another of her owners, John Quiller the *Swallow* took an unarmed French coaster *Le Sage Alexis* in the Bay of Biscay and four days later, a Spanish merchant vessel bound for Philadelphia, the *El San Louis De Bilbao*.

When a fourth prize, the *St. Anne D'Arson* was taken early in 1783, Job advertised the sale of all four vessels, together with their cargo, in the *Sherborne & Yeovil Mercury*.

The sale was held on the afternoon of Monday, March 3rd 1783, at the New Inn on the quay at Polperro. Such an event caused quite a stir in the area, attracting a large crowd of curious onlookers and prospective buyers to the harbour where three of the vessels seized by the *Swallow* were berthed; the big *San Louis De Bilbao* remained at Fowey where she had been taken following her capture.

The *St. Anne D'Arson* was sold for £130, her cargo of wine having been previously sold at Guernsey for nearly the same amount. The privateer *Le Chardon* fetched only £63, while the *El San Louis De Bilbao* and her cargo of wine, brandy and cloth was sold for £482 and the 38 tons of yellow rosin from the *Sage Alexis*, much sought-after for soap and medicines, raised a further £554. Even after Job had deducted his own and other expences incurred in claiming the *Swallow's* prizes her owners must have been satisfied with the outcome of their privateering ventures.

In due course, Job applied to the Mayor of Plymouth for the £5 head money paid for every enemy prisoner captured at sea due on the 16 crewmen from the prize *Le Chardon*, adding a further £80 to the proceeds of the *Swallow's* success. Such bounty money encouraged the taking of prisoners alive instead of some excuse being found to kill or drown them.

When the war with France and Spain ended early in 1783 the *Swallow* was compelled to abandon her lucrative privateering activity and return instead to the smuggling trade under the command of William Johns, a 40-year-old Polperro mariner and associate of John Quiller. Her luck ran out in April as she lay becalmed at anchor by Lundy Island, a notorious haven for smugglers that lay a few miles off the North Devon coast in the Bristol Channel.

While a party of the *Swallow's* crew, including William Johns, was ashore on the island making contact with the handful of inhabitants who survived there by selling contraband liquor to passing fishermen, a naval man-of-war HMS *Beaver* was observed approaching from the north. The alarm was raised and, while the shore party scrambled down the steep narrow cliff path that led to their boat, panic broke out among those aboard the lugger as they cut the anchor cable and tried to get under way despite the absence of wind.

Under the cover of darkness, those aboard the *Swallow* did everything possible to get in as close to the north Devon coast as possible, out of sight of the man-of-war that had meanwhile dropped anchor near the island. But at daybreak the following morning they found to their dismay they were still in sight of the *Beaver*, a 14-gun sloop commanded by Captain Joseph Peyton whose log for Friday April 18th 1783 recorded laconically:

> *Fired several guns to bring to the lugger. Hauled with our pinnace and boats, gave chase, rowed with the sweeps.* At 4 came to an anchor. Manned and armed the boats and gave chase. At 6 the boats boarded her, Hartland Point SSE 3 or 4 miles, found her to be the Swallow from Guernsey loaded with Tea, Brandy and Gin belonging to Polperro.*

Without a breath of wind to assist them, the Polperro crew stood little chance of escaping the heavily-armed sloop being steadily hauled towards them by its crew and boats; after about six hours of desperately pulling on the lugger's sweeps they were eventually overhauled and boarded without a fight.

The *Swallow* was loaded with 119 sacks of Bohea tea, 242 barrels of brandy and 90 barrels of gin altogether worth nearly £2,000. Since no papers could be produced to account for such a cargo, it was correctly assumed to be contraband. Caught in the very act of smuggling, crew, cargo and vessel were impounded by the *Beaver* and ordered to sail under escort for Plymouth the following day. While the *Swallow* had been attempting to escape, one of her crew had managed to get ashore at Hartland Point on the mainland and make his way to Polperro. As soon as news of the *Swallow*'s seizure reached Job he set out immediately for Plymouth with John Quiller and began once again the process of securing her release.

This time, however, the evidence against the *Swallow* was overwhelming. Job and Quiller would have watched with growing consternation as their vessel was brought into Plymouth Sound under naval escort and handed over to the

---

* Sweeps were long, heavy oars carried by sailing vessels for use when the wind failed.

Collector of Customs. For the next nine months, Job spared no effort to pursue a claim for the return of the *Swallow* and her cargo, procuring witnesses, instructing lawyers and travelling twice to London to attend the trial at Westminster Hall. In all, he made nearly 40 entries in his ledger in 1783 under the heading 'disbursements on the *Swallow* when seized by Captain Peyton' relating to expenses incurred by him amounting to more than £191. This total was shared by the *Swallow* owners who now included James Tinney, Petherick Lukey and Mrs Susanna Hockins.

If the profits from smuggling were large, so too were the risks and losses. The loss of the *Swallow* and her valuable cargo was a severe blow to the lugger's owners, even to Zephaniah Job who at that time was still impatiently awaiting the proceeds from the capture of the *Rusee* several years earlier. The peace with France had brought an end to privateering and with it, Job's run of success until an unexpected development occurred that was to do more to establish his reputation as a man of business than any amount of financial fortune.

5

Trelawny Steward

A few days after Zephaniah Job's 36th birthday at the beginning of 1786 a letter arrived unexpectedly at his home in Polperro from the local squire, the Reverend Sir Harry Trelawny, inviting Job to become his steward.

Sir Harry Trelawny had inherited his baronetcy and the family estate at Trelawne* in the neighbouring parish of Pelynt above Polperro in 1772 at the age of 16 on the death of his father, then Governor of Jamaica. The young Sir Harry was more interested in religion than riches and in due course became ordained as an Anglican minister at Exeter, leaving the management of his estates in Cornwall in the hands of others.

Job gladly accepted the baronet's offer at once without even agreeing a salary, replying only that he would 'cheerfully accept such terms as shall meet your Honour's approbation.' The delight and pride he felt at being appointed by this 'very ancient and respectable family' as he referred to the Trelawnys, was soon tempered by the knowledge that Sir Harry's affairs were badly in need of financial management.

Sir Harry was one of the greatest landowners in the neighbourhood of Polperro, with hundreds of acres of rich farm and woodland to the west of Looe as well as land and property elsewhere in Cornwall in the hands of his many tenants.

---

* Trelawne was bought by Sir John Trelawny in 1600 and rebuilt by Bishop Sir Jonathan Trelawny at the beginning of the 18th century. It was acquired from the Trelawny family in the 1940s and is now a holiday site.

Although he had a keen and enquiring mind, taking great interest in new farming developments, not everything he did met with the approval of his employees and neighbours. One of his first acts on moving into Trelawne had been to order the destruction of all the old formal gardens, fountains and fish ponds as well as the magnificent Gothic gate-house and the fine library of books it contained. Not surprisingly, local people often referred to him as 'Mad Sir Harry.'

The manor of Trelawne was a fine Gothic mansion set in several acres of parkland with a commanding view of the coast. Approached by a tree-lined avenue, its most striking features were a battlemented tower and adjoining chapel. Sir Harry's devotion to his religious activities left little time for the care of domestic and other matters, and on arrival at Trelawne Job found much evidence of mismanagement, waste and debt when he took over the administration of the estates and household, including the affairs of Lady Anne Trelawny and her six children.

A few months after Job's arrival, Sir Harry travelled to Paris where he remained for several weeks, leaving his new steward with full authority to make whatever economies were necessary. All expenditure was scrutinised, all wages and allowances of employees examined and all transactions punctiliously entered by Job in his own distinctive hand at the top of each ledger page under the heading: *The Reverend Sir Harry Trelawny Bart. in A/C with Zephaniah Job*.

One of his first measures was to reduce the wages of those members of staff who, like the gardener and his family, had been receiving substantial benefits in kind from the estate. He also proposed cutting the number of staff by dismissing two maidservants. Sir Harry had left instructions that all expenditure was to be handled by Job; even Lady Trelawny had to ask for money for herself. On one occasion, soon after Sir Harry's departure, learning that Lady Trelawny had ordered a set of new chairs for the hall at Trelawne, Job was obliged to tell her he could not pay any more accounts that had not first been agreed by Sir Harry. Job's diplomatic skills in dealing with such delicate domestic issues were certainly demanded when it came to reducing Lady Trelawny's own household outgoings. And when he wrote to Sir Harry reporting on progress, he invariably adopted a tone of deference bordering on servility:

> 'I cannot thank your Honour for the satisfaction you have been pleased to express on my management of your affairs. I shall make it the study of my life to deserve your Honour's approbation. I remain with the greatest esteem and respect, Honoured and Reverend Sir Your Honour's most devoted, most obedient and very humble servant,
>   Zephaniah Job

In August 1786, the baronet sent word from the Hotel de Luxembourg in Paris where he was staying for his house-steward William Wills to join him. Wills had managed the Trelawny accounts until Job's arrival, and had continued to attend to some of the day-to-day matters involving the Trelawne household under Job's direction. Job duly wrote a letter of introduction to Nicholas Maingy & Brothers, one of the Guernsey merchants with whom he dealt on behalf of the Polperro smugglers, asking them to issue Wills with a credit note for £50 and assist him in travelling on to Paris via the French port of Roscoff.

Suffering from indifferent health and unwilling to face the rigours of another wet winter in Cornwall, Sir Harry remained abroad until the following year, corresponding regularly with his steward who in turn continued to send lengthy reports of the economies introduced at Trelawne, describing in considerable detail the measures taken to improve the management of the Trelawne estates and increase the income from them. When there were problems with the staff at Trelawne in Sir Harry's continued absence, Job kept his master fully informed.

When an affair between the farm manager at Trelawne, a man named Fairweather, and one of the female servants began to cause domestic difficulties, Job reported:

'Conjecture that the lovers' time would be wholly taken up in admiring each other was well founded. Since your absence it has been abundantly so, and in consequence of sitting up late are sometimes not downstairs in the morning till 8 or 9 o'clock. Molly told Mr Fairweather it was shameful for him to be in bed so late when so many men had been long waiting his orders. This incurred his high displeasure. Kicks and blows were threatened and barely prevented. Your Honour must be fully convinced under the present circumstances, the sooner Mr Fairweather leaves Trelawne the more it will be for your interest.'

Job's wish to be rid of Fairweather was granted a few months later when the man eventually left Trelawne, paid off with two year's salary, and William Wills was appointed farm manager in his place.

In the summer of 1786 a miner from Helston, Robert Smithem, approached Job and announced he had found a rich vein of lead ore running onto part of the Trelawne estate. The discovery was near an abandoned mine-working known today as Herodsfoot about five miles up the West Looe river that marked the boundary of Sir Harry's land. When he examined the samples of ore that Smithem had brought him, Job at once recognised them to be of top quality lead-bearing deposits that could, in all probability, be easily extracted. The knowledge and experience gained during his earlier years in St. Agnes quickly persuaded him that such a discovery on the Trelawne estate would add considerably to the value of the land as well as provide a useful source of revenue.

Smithem's purpose in revealing his find to Job had been to obtain a licence to extract the ore at Herodsfoot. Instead, Job told him that no licence would be granted and even warned the miner that he would be prosecuted if he attempted to work any land belonging to the Trelawne estate. Job meanwhile wrote to Sir Harry :

'I would advise to work the mine immediately on your account with a few gentlemen whom you might wish should have shares or parts in the said adventure; I would gladly venture a part myself.'

In due course, Smithem was granted a licence in return for a substantial share of the proceeds and Job accordingly drew up the following agreement:

I Zephaniah Job Steward & Attorney to Sir Harry Trelawny Bt. do hereby for one Moiety [half share] grant Licence to Robert Smithem and his adventurers to try for Tin Lead & Copper that he shall or may discover in a certain estate called Botelet Woods at Herierdsfoot & will grant him a deed for the Moiety to work the same Reserving the one eighth dish [royalty] as soon as applied for and also reserving such part as the Lords or the said Z. Job may choose to adventure.

Job's confidence in the venture initially seemed misplaced, for some two years later he felt obliged to mention in the course of one of his reports to Sir Harry abroad:

'The mine goes on at Herierdsfoot. An engine is now at work drawing the water out of the old bottoms, but no discovery yet made...'*

In due course, Job was able to tell Sir Harry that Lady Trelawny 'and your fine little family are perfectly well and have adopted a plan of economy,' adding also: 'I shall do all in my power to observe frugality in every department.'

Lady Trelawny eventually joined her husband in Paris for Easter in 1788, taking her two daughters with her. John Trelawny, the eldest of their four sons, had just started at Westminster school in London at the age of eight, leaving his younger brother William at school in Truro where he was

---

* In 1850 the Mining Journal reported that the sale of lead ore from the lead mines of Herodsfoot and Trelawne had increased rapidly, reaching the level of the neighbouring copper mines to the north of Liskeard.

visited by Job. School fees were yet another of Sir Harry's expenses taken care of by his steward.

Sir Harry's prolonged stay abroad made the task of reforming the Trelawne affairs even more difficult. Many of the measures Job wished to implement required his master's assent, and each of his proposals had to be explained at length by correspondence between them. From time to time Job would express concern at Sir Harry's continued absence, as on one occasion:

'The loss which I must experience by your Honour's absence is evident, besides as my highest friend and counsellor, I shall often be straightened not knowing how to act for want of your presence to direct me.'

The extent of Sir Harry's financial difficulties is best illustrated by the fact that he was compelled to borrow substantially from his steward, as much as £4,000 in 1788, just two years after Job's appointment to the Trelawny family. Even by the end of 1787, Sir Harry was £1,081 in debt to Job; a year later this had increased to £1,510 and Job recorded in his ledger 'Sir Harry gave me his note of hand for part of the above balance £1,000.' In ten years Sir Harry's debt rose to more than £5,000 and was only eventually repaid twenty years later, during which time Job's salary of £50 a year and interest at 4 1/2% was added by accrual.*

Having obtained an IOU for £500, Job was obviously content to let his master's debit balance increase by as much as ten times the original debt, secure in the knowledge that the law allowed a creditor to secure the arrest and imprisonment of anyone whose note of hand he held. It was to prove a significant factor in Job's role as banker to both squirearchy and smugglers alike.

---

* Sir Harry Trelawny's debit account with job continued until 1807 when part of the Trelawny estate at Bochym near Helston was sold by Sir Harry to his son William Lewis for £9,000. With the proceeds he was able to repay the £3,000 mortgage on Bochym and the £5,000 or so he owed Job and others.

Sir Harry eventually returned home to Cornwall in the summer of 1788, but his continued ill-health compelled him to return to the Continent again in October, this time to Vevey, a popular health resort on the northern shores of Lake Geneva where he remained until Christmas that year.

Job's efforts to improve the productivity of the Trelawny estates had far-reaching effects on the neighbouring rural economy. New breeds of cattle were introduced, largely encouraged by Sir Harry's association with Robert Bakewell, the noted Leicestershire cattle breeder. Traditionally, sand and seaweed had been used to manure the fields; for centuries oxen and horses had hauled sleds laden with it from the shore to the farms. Job bought lime from Looe and dung from Polperro and had it ploughed into the soil of the Trelawne fields to improve the harvest yield. He also employed men and boys to collect dung from the surrounding area. This was carried out on such a scale that he was even appointed the official Scavenger for East Looe. There was more than a hint of self-mocking irony when he broke the news of his appointment in a letter to Sir Harry in Switzerland:

'You will I hope give me joy as I begin first to fill a mean office. I may possibly one day be promoted.'

Sir Harry's visits to Europe continued despite the outbreak of war with revolutionary France in 1793, on one occasion returning via the Italian port of Leghorn aboard the brig *Richard and Mary* hired by Job to ship a cargo of pilchards from Polperro. With French naval ships lurking in the Mediterranean, such a voyage would have been fraught with danger.

Back at Trelawne, meanwhile, the bills continued to mount up, despite Job's efforts to curtail expenditure. More often than not, his frequent admonitions went unheeded. Lady Trelawny spent much of her time in London, school bills had to be paid as well as wages for the large household at Trelawne and more than once Job felt compelled to warn his master of the need for economy:

'Bills for Trelawne are running on your account at the different shops in Looe, Liskeard and Plymouth to a large amount. During your absence, and while the family remain in London, this should be made an end of entirely. The servants that remain at Trelawne should be placed on board wages and a fixed sum, whatever you please, be given to Mr Wills. By this means you will know your expenditure which on the present plan is much more considerable than you are aware of.'

By the end of 1795, Job had persuaded Sir Harry and his wife that their house-steward, William Wills must also go and that a further £600 a year could be saved if Lady Trelawny were to give up the London home at Queen Square in Bloomsbury she delighted in spending so much time at with her children and return to live at Trelawne. Wills was evidently reluctant to move from the comfortable surroundings of Trelawne that he and his wife had enjoyed for so many years, especially while Sir Harry and his family were absent. When Wills protested that he could not leave until Lady Trelawny arrived from London, Job even offered to move in himself. Eventually William Wills and his wife were settled in Plymouth early in 1796 and later that year Sir Harry and his family were reunited at Trelawne.

Sir Harry's eldest son John joined the Navy on leaving school, serving in the West Indies aboard *HMS Dictator* where he was later promoted to Lieutenant. When John Trelawny's younger brother William Lewis went up to Oriel College, Oxford, after leaving Westminster School, Job opened a separate account for the young undergraduate on his father's instructions:

'Having received a letter from Sir Harry Trelawny ordering me to charge all monies which I have advanced to Mr William Lewis since he left Westminster to his own separate account, it will stand as under, viz:

1799		£
Jan 17	To cash at Mr Rice's at East Looe	1..1..
Mar 28	To the Rev Dr Cooke at Oriel College Oxford for your entrance	22.. ..
Apr 1	To cash to yourself for your journey to Oxford and to pay expences there	30.. ..
Apr 16	Remittance to you at Oriel College	40.. ..
June 1	To do. " " do.	30.. ..
July 5	To cash advanced you at Trelawny	5..5..
Aug 15	To cash sent you by William Jay from East Looe	10.10..
Aug 31	To remittance to Dr Glass for part of Oriels (a tailors) bill by your order	25.. ..
Sep 11	To cash and bank notes advanced you at Polperro to pay your bills at Oxford	70.. ..
Oct 3	To remittance to you at Stoke	40.. ..
Nov 8	To do. at Oriel College	20.. ..
Dec 21	To do. at do.	50.. ..
Dec 30	To R.Crisp bill for shoes and boots	3..18..6
		£347.14..

Job's stewardship for William Lewis Trelawny, for which he received an annual salary of twenty guineas, extended over a number of years in the course of which the young man took the family name Salusbury under the will of his cousin. In November 1802 Job debits him £115 as William Lewis Salusbury Esq. 'for changing your name'. The high fee was for the cost of obtaining a royal licence through the College of Arms. At the time of his marriage to the daughter of John Phillipps Carpenter in 1807, he had become William Lewis Salusbury-Trelawny, later inheriting the baronetcy on the death of his father in 1834.*

In later years, Job continued to manage Sir Harry's affairs and those of other members of the Trelawny family. The

---

* William Lewis, later Sir William Lewis Salusbury-Trelawny, having taken the name Salusbury under the will of his cousin Owen Salusbury Brereton, married Patience Carpenter in 1807, became High Sheriff of Cornwall in 1811 and later Lord Lieutenant of the county between 1839-1856.

threat of invasion from Napoleon's armies at the end of the eighteenth century was such that all manner of measures were undertaken by the government in Britain. Local militia and Sea Fencibles were formed, naval shipbuilding was increased and additional taxes were imposed on a wide range of luxury goods to pay for it all. There was a tax on windows, a tax on horses, a tax on servants, a land tax, a house tax, a property tax, a dog tax and even a hairpowder tax.* For a large household like Trelawne, as Job's ledgers show, the annual tax bill was considerable, rising from £41 in 1797 to nearly £79 in 1803.

By the time the wars with France had finally ended with Napoleon's defeat at Waterloo, Job had become more of a family friend and confidant, regularly calling at Trelawne and taking tea with Sir Harry and other members of the household.

Sir Harry's youngest daughter Mary, who continued to live at Trelawne with her husband John Cooke Harding and their four children while they looked for somewhere to live, refers frequently to Job's visits in her diary between 1813 and 1817. The Hardings needed the financial help of both Sir Harry and Job, but this proved elusive and the period was an unhappy one for Mary although she was a frequent visitor to Job's house in Polperro where she sought his advice, recording on one occasion: 'Mr Job is quite cheering, sees everything in bright colours.'

Mary continued to fret at Trelawne until Job arranged for the Hardings to be taken across to France in August 1814 aboard the *Polperro*, a schooner owned by him whose captain was the same John Clements who had been one of his pupils forty years earlier. When they returned in April the following year from Guernsey, Mary described how her father was waiting on the quay to meet them:

---

* In April 1798 Job debited Sir Harry Trelawny's account with the following entry: To Hairpowder Licences for My Lady, Sir Harry, Miss Trelawny and James Rendle, £4.4s.

'We sailed down with a brisk wind to Polperro. Boats soon came out but the horrid custom house officers made a fuss about our landing as the vessel was not cleared for this port. This was a mystery the captain would not tell us about. The dear Sir came himself to meet us, he was one of the first I saw after Mr Couch;* came up to Mr Job's with him quite overcome, but got better afterwards.'

Despite the apparent vigilance of the Customs officials at Polperro on that occasion, Mary Harding's occasional references to the smugglers in her diary not only make it clear that contraband was still being shipped across the Channel after the Napoleonic wars but it was also common knowledge even to the Trelawny family:

Friday 28th June 1816. Trelawne.
'Wrote to my Ed and in the evening the smuggler called saying he was going to sail for Roscoff at 12 o'clock tonight. Gave him my letter. A very civil man - talked with him and should have heard more but Sir H came and called me....'

There are numerous entries in Job's ledgers debiting Sir Harry Trelawny's account for payments for spirits to the Polperro smugglers, as in April 1796:

The Revd. Sir Harry Trelawny Bart   *Dr.*
To William Johns for Brandy & Gin   10..10..

Similar payments were made to John Quiller and Richard Barrett. There is even an entry crediting Sir Harry with 18 shillings from 'Joseph Turner for 2/3 of a six gallon cask of brandy taken up on Talland beach after allowing him 1/3 for salvage.' No doubt the cask had been run ashore at Talland, having been shipped over from Guernsey by one of the smugglers in the first place.

---

* Dr. Jonathan Couch (1789-1870), Polperro physician, naturalist and grandfather of the author Sir Arthur Quiller Couch.

There is ample evidence that the Reverend Sir Harry Trelawny, head of one of Cornwall's foremost families and a member of the magistracy, was a willing accomplice in defrauding the Revenue by buying direct from the smugglers.

The Rev. Sir Harry Trelawny (1777)
(Courtesy of the National Portrait Gallery, London)

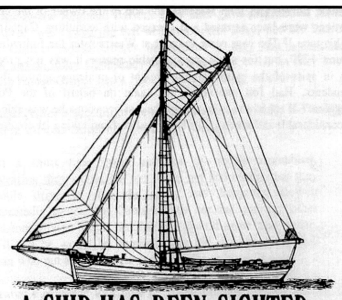

A SHIP HAS BEEN SIGHTED

in this quarter

ENGAGING IN THE UNLAWFUL ACT OF

SMUGGLING

whosoever can lay information
leading to the capture of this ship
or its crew

will receive a reward of

£500

From His Majesty's Government

This 19th day of October 1782

Customs poster 1782

William Quiller's smuggling jug

Revenue cutter c1810
(Thomas Whitcombe RA - NMM)

Gabriel Bray self-portrait (1775)
(National Maritime Museum, London)

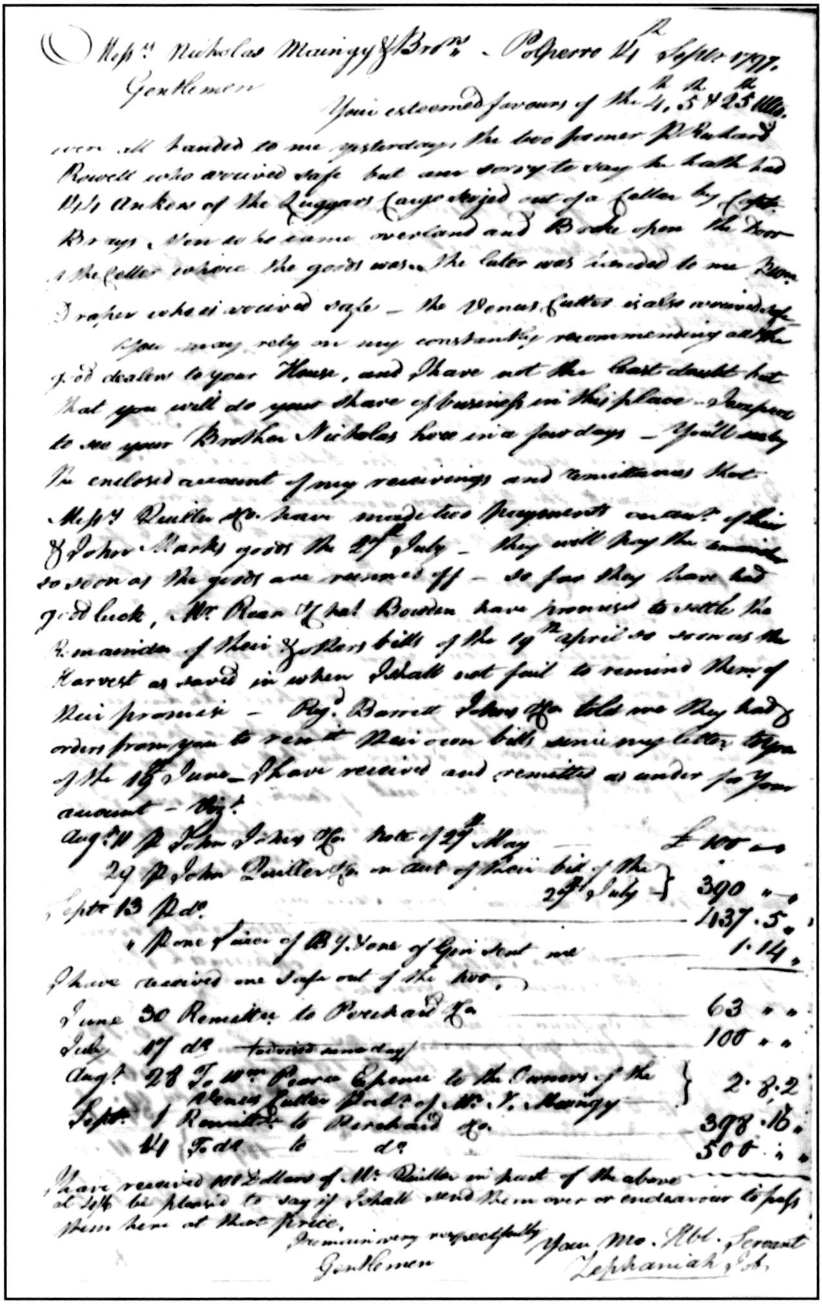
Messrs Nicholas Maingy & Brors – Polperro 14th Septr 1797.

Gentlemen

Your esteemed favours of the 4th, 5th & 25th Ulto. were all handed to me yesterday, the two former by Richard Rowett who arrived safe but am sorry to say he hath had [illegible] Ankers of the Luggars Cargo seized out of a Cellar by Captn Brays. [illegible] came overland and Broke open the Door of the Cellar where the goods was. The latter was handed to me by Wm Draper who is arrived safe – the Venus Cutter is also arrived safe.

You may rely on my constantly recommending all the good dealers to your House, and I have not the least doubt but that you will do your share of business in this place. I expect to see your Brother Nicholas here in a few days – You'll see by the enclosed account of my receivings and remittances that Messrs Quiller &c. have made two payments on account of their & John Marks goods the 27th July – they will pay the remainder so soon as the goods are runned off – so far they have had good luck. Mr Rean & Nathl Bowden have promised to settle the Remainder of their & others bills of the 19th April so soon as the Harvest is saved in when I shall not fail to remind them of their promise – Richd Barrett Jobns &c told me they had orders from you to remit their own bills since my letter to you of the 19th June – I have received and remitted as under for your account – Vizt

Augt 11	by John Jobns &c Note of 27 May	£ 100 – –
29	by John Quiller &c on acct of their bill of the 27th July	390 – –
Septr 13	by do.	437.5.–
	by one piece of B.Y. [illegible] of Geo. Hext [illegible]	1.14.–
	I have received one [illegible] out of the [illegible]	
June 30	Remitted to Perchard &c	63 – –
July 17	do. [illegible]	100 – –
Augt 28	To Wm Pearce Expence to the Owners of the Venus Cutter by order of Mr N. Maingy	2.8.2
Septr 1	Remitted to Perchard &c	398.16.–
14	To do. to do.	500 – –

I have received 100 Dollars of Mr Quiller in part of the above at 4/6 be pleased to say if I shall send them over or endeavour to pass them here at that price.

I remain very respectfully
Gentlemen
Your mo. Obt. Servant
Zephaniah Job.

Job letter to Messrs Nicholas Maingy & Bros. (1797)

(Royal Institution of Cornwall)

1794

Mar. 1 Ashburton 30 Michl. Moon Walton & per Greens Will & Son

" 10 Falmouth 30 Robert Hicks Geo. C. & x W Srs. Roberts, Curtis

" " do " Peter Johns do. Esdaile & Co

" " do " John Kendall do do

Decr. 10 London note of J. Tonkin

1794 Mar. 21 Looe 30 Zephh. Job Job & Co & & Adams & Hodge

15 Fowey 40 & & & Tickett W.G. Carter Fry & Son & Co

3 Bucklandland 30 do B. Adams M.G.K. Moore

27 Bristol 2 Mo. Job & Grigg Robt. Castle & Co. I. Oliver, Skett

April 5 Portsm. 30 Mess. Tickett W.G. Carter Fry & Son & Co

" 7 Ply Dock 30 John Clements John Elworthy Hen: Landys Esq

" 10 St. Austle 30 Z, Job Chris. Parnell Wm Banks
Kingston Buildings

Mar. 25 Zephy. Bk, demand & J, Bennett. Wm Clarke & Sons Sir James Esdaile

April 16 Portsm. 30 Job & Grigg Saml. Wheeler Peter Tormans
= Coffee Office: Red Bull Wharf - upper Thames Street - Lon

Mar. 22 North Tawton 30 Henry Sargent Char. Sweet John & Philip Perrin

" 17 London Bearer For the Govr. & Compa. Bank of England
H. Threlkeld

April 12 Polperro 30 John Avent John Mackenzie Thos. Bryer

" 26 Crediton 30 James Nicholas R. Abraham Burlenwood & Yeath

May 3 do. 30 do. John Welsford I. Commerell & Lubb
& Co

" 3 do. 30 do. Thomas Madge John & Philip Perrin

" 6 Bristol 2 mo. Job & Grigg Rob Castle & Co. I. Oliver. Skett & Co

" 3 Trehane 30 Henry Pooley Will Stackhouse Brook Watson & Co

" 13 Looe 30 Rich. Wm Gwennap Job & Grigg Adams & Hodge

" 13 do. 30 Dobree & Aubin do. do.

Extract from Zephaniah Job's Banking List (1794)
(Royal Institution of Cornwall)

74.

Date	Name	Payee	No.	£ s d
Jan. 10	Rich.ᵈ Rowett & Co.	Chas. Kendall		£ 20 " "
18	Rob.ᵗ Hicks	Do.		10 10 "
20	Jno. Johns	Mr. DeLisle		23 19 9
"	John Kendall	Thomson & Son		20 " "
	Wm. Johns	do.		5 5 "
21	. . . .	Dobree & Aubin		95 3 9
"	J. & J. Tibbett & Co.	Porchard & Brock 1255		200 " "
"	do.	Do. Do. 137		100 " "
29	Michael Castle	Porchard & Brock		574 " "
Feb. 11	Thos. & Steph.ᵉ Tibbett	Wm. Johns 1437		147 17 "
"	John Clemens	Tho. May do.		50 " "
		do.		100 " "
Apr. 12	Thwaites & Bennett			2105 4 16 1
" 19	Sam.ˡ Wheeler 15/May	Porchard & Brock		304 10 "
May 2	John Sangmaid 25 Apl.	do. do.		20 " "
do.	do.	Thos. Oxland	980	5 " "
do.	do. 15 May	Porchard & Brock		20 " "
do.	do. 29 do.	Thos. Oxland		30 " "
do.	do. 3/6 June	Porchard & Brock		20 " "
do.	do. 3/6 do.	do. do.	31	20 " "
" 9	Michael Castle & Co.	Dan.ˡ DeLisle Esqr.		290 7 "
do.	Wm. Pooley 3/6 June	do.		25 18 6
	10/16 do.	Rob.ᵗ & Wm. Gummoe		8 17 6

Extract from Zephaniah Job's Banking List (1794)
(Royal Institution of Cornwall)

2 0 June. 1803.

Appeared personally *Irving Brock of Bumfordland Broadstone Street London Gentleman*

(on Behalf of William Johns now at Looe in the County of Cornwall) —
and produced a Warrant from the Right Honourable the Lords Commissioners for executing the Office of Lord High Admiral of the United
Kingdom of *Great Britain* and *Ireland*, &c. for the granting of Letters
of Marque and Reprisals to him the said *William Johns*
for the apprehending, seizing, and taking the Ships, Vessels, and Goods,
belonging to the *French Republic*, or to any Persons being Subjects of
the *French Republic*, or inhabiting within any of the Territories of the
French Republic, and in pursuance of His Majesty's Instructions, made
the following Declaration, *(to wit.)* That his the said *William Johns'*
Ship is called the *Industry* — — is
belonging to the *Port of Looe in Cornwall* is of the Burthen of
about eighty five — Tons, *is a square sterned clinker cutter fitted as a Sloop with a plain stem and*
has *one* — Mast, that the said *William Johns*
goeth Commander of her, that she is mounted with *six*
Carriage Guns, carrying Shot of *1, 1·1/2, & 2* —Pounds Weight,
and *four* — — — Swivel Guns, is navigated with *thirty six*
— — Men, of whom One-Third are Landmen, has *twenty*
Small Arms, *thirty* — Cutlasses, *twenty* —
Barrels of Powder, *fifty* — Rounds of Great Shot, and
about *two hundred* —Weight of Small Shot, that the said Ship
is victualled for *three* — Months, has *three* — Suits
of Sails, *three* — Anchors, *three* — Cables, and about
five hundred Weight of Spare Cordage, that *James —
Ellis* — — goeth Mate, or Lieutenant, *George Rose*
— — — Gunner, *William Pitt* Boatswain, *John —
Canning* —Carpenter, *Henry Addington* Cook,
and *William Windham* Surgeon, of the said Ship,
and that *Zephaniah Job of the Parish
of Talland in the County of Cornwall
is the sole* — — —

Owner and Setter-out of the said Ship.

Irving Brock.

On the same Day
This Declaration was made
Before Me

Application for *Industry* Letter of Marque (1803)
(National Archives, London)

6

The Quillers

Zephaniah Job's association with the Trelawny family afforded him the very respectability and influence he required in an age when social connections and class were of great importance in matters of business and dealings with those in positions of authority. Yet it was his links with the Quiller family of Polperro that were to provide the foundation for his eventual wealth.

The Quillers were descended from French émigrés who came to East Cornwall during the 17th century. One branch of the family settled in Lansallos where John Quiller was born in 1741, growing up to become one of the sea-going fraternity who earned their living by fishing and whatever other opportunities presented themselves. By the time of Job's arrival in Polperro, Quiller had gained a formidable reputation as a buccaneering and fearless figure on land and sea.

John Quiller married a local girl, Jane Libby, in 1763 and the couple had ten children including three sons: Richard, William and John, all of whom were to play an active part in their father's smuggling and privateering activities. Their father owned several boats, among them the *Swallow*, *Alert* and the *Brilliant*, which he fitted out for privateering the moment war broke out.

It was John Quiller's joint ownership of the *Swallow* that led to his lifelong association with Zephaniah Job upon whom he depended for the administration of his complex smuggling and privateering ventures. Job's tenacious pursuit of the proceeds of the *Swallow*'s prize, *Rusee*, was to forge an enduring bond of friendship between the two men for nearly 25 years.

The *Brilliant*, a three-masted lugger of 120 tons was, like the smaller *Swallow*, one of the most successful Cornish privateers to venture against shipping of Britain's enemies at the time. As with others, ownership of the *Brilliant* was divided among several shareholders including Zephaniah Job and John Quiller senior. Job kept detailed records of payments both made and received in connection with the vessel, including an inventory he drew up in September 1786 when he wrote to one of his London agents, Paul Le Mesurier offering a £400 share in the *Brilliant*:

> *Hull, Masts, Yards, Standing and Running Rigging good as she came in from sea.*
> *1 Large Mainsail*
> *1 Great Foresail*
> *1 Trysail*
> *1 Main Topsail*
> *1 Working Foresail to ye fore Mast*
> *1 Maccarony foresail*
> *2 Storme foresails*
> *1 for topsail*
> *4 Jibbs*
> *3 Mizzens*
> *2 Cables almost new & 2 Ankers good*
> *1 Copper Kettle*
> *1 do. Teakettle*
> *2 Brass Compasses*
> *with sundry other stores belong to the said Luggar Brilliant*

A month later Job noted that he had sold to John Quiller and another of the Polperro smugglers, William Johns, his own quarter share in the *Swallow* and *Brilliant* for £197..10s. When the *Brilliant* was eventually sold to a group of Guernsey shipowners and merchants in 1793 for £2,000, Quiller collected a share of the proceeds.*

* The *Brilliant* was eventually captured by the French in October 1793 and taken into service with the French navy until 1799

Among the many prizes seized by the *Brilliant* was the 200 ton Spanish ship *La Tortola* which, when sold by order of the High Court of Admiralty, yielded the astonishing sum of £8,800 for the crew and her owners. Privateer crews generally received no wages while they were at sea; instead, the proceeds were divided between the owners of the vessel and the ship's company, with each crew member owning an agreed share in the venture. In the case of the *Brilliant*, John Quiller senior held a quarter share as part owner along with Job, who held an eighth. In addition, Quiller held a further 64 shares as captain of the vessel.

The application to the Admiralty Court was handled by Guernsey merchants Lessier & Wood. Job wrote to them in 1795, a year after the *Brilliant* had been sold, enclosing instructions he had drafted on behalf of John Quiller senior and his sons William and John:

'Be pleased to settle with Mr Job for 1/4 and 1/64 part of the privateer the Brilliant's prize La Tortola and my 64 shares as captain of the said privateer, also for my son William's 40 shares and my son John's 32 shares.'

Unable to read or write, Quiller signed the note with just his initials, witnessed by Job's 19-year-old nephew Zephaniah, employed at the time as his uncle's clerk. As the *Brilliant's* commander, John Quiller's share of the proceeds amounted to £1,100, while Job received £550 and Quiller's sons William and John their proportion each. Such prize money made the physical and financial risks involved in privateering seem small by comparison.

Not long afterwards, Richard, the eldest of the three Quiller brothers, was lost at sea at the age of 33 leaving Job with the task of settling his affairs. He was the father of seven children, including two sets of twin girls, several of whom had died in infancy. In later years, his grandson Thomas Quiller Couch recalled how Richard Quiller would hang the key of his quadrant on a beam at his home in Polperro before putting to sea with a stern warning that no one was touch it until he returned. After his death in 1796, the 'tragic key' as it became known, remained where he had left it for many years in deference to his wish.

Richard's father owned a small lugger which he named the *Three Brothers* after his sons. He had bought the boat from the Customs who had probably seized it for smuggling, only to find he was refused the necessary licence to take it to sea. Job took the matter up on his behalf, pointing out that the vessel was sold by order of His Majesty's Customs and could not proceed to sea without first taking out a licence:

'If none can be had, pray what could be the intention of such a sale or what is Mr Quiller to do with the vessel?.'

John Quiller senior had obviously incurred the displeasure or suspicion of the Customs who were probably not convinced that the new owner of the *Three Brothers* had no connection with the contraband trade. As a result of Job's intervention, the vessel was eventually permitted to put to sea, only to be lost several years later.

The sea took a terrible toll of the Quillers, claiming the lives of many of the male members of the family with whom Job associated. After Richard's death in 1796, tragedy struck again when his father John was drowned during a severe gale off the north coast of Cornwall. In November 1804 the *Sherborne Mercury* carried the following report:

'A melancholy accident happened at Porth Just cove in the parish of St Just in Penwith, Cornwall, on Sunday the 4th by the upsetting of a boat that was coming from a smuggling lugger lying off the cove in which were eight men; when the boat came within twenty yards of the shore a heavy surf overtook and completely overturned her and three only out of the eight were saved. The unfortunate sufferers were chiefly young men belonging to the lugger and inhabitants of Polperro.'

The bodies of three of the men who drowned that day were later washed ashore. Two of them, Richard Toms and Richard Richards, were from Polperro. The third was Thomas Hicks, the innkeeper at St Just who had evidently collected £100 in bank notes and other bills to pay for goods from the Polperro boat lying offshore in Priest's Cove.

Whether as a result of this incident or another that month, John Quiller's body was later brought ashore at Newquay and Job arranged for the funeral expences to be paid, including the sum of £3 for brandy! He had been appointed by John Quiller as his executor of the will he had drawn up only a year or so before his death:

I do hereby constitute and appoint my friend Mr Zephaniah Job of Polperro sole executor in trust for the execution and performance of this my last will and testament...

Accordingly, Job ensured that John Quiller's widow Mary and his surviving daughters Jane and Elizabeth were provided for from their father's considerable assets. Elizabeth inherited the family home in Polperro on condition she allowed her mother to remain there, while her sister Jane was left a house next to the lime kilns overlooking the harbour. Other property belonging to him was divided among the various children of his son Richard who had died several years earlier.

Richard Quiller's younger brother William was actively engaged in smuggling from an early age. He was only 22 when he was in command of the *Vigilant*, a fishing boat belonging to his father, which was seized by the Revenue cutter *Constitution* during the night of June 24th, 1797. The *Constitution*'s commander, Lieutenant John Weston had good reason to suspect that a Polperro boat was quite likely to be carrying more than just a cargo of fish, but on this occasion he was unlucky. Although no contraband goods were found aboard her, the *Vigilant* was brought into Falmouth under escort. Job at once sent a note with William's father to James Tippett, a Falmouth lawyer, instructing him to enter a claim for it to be returned to its owners:

'Captain Weston can have no right whatever to detain this vessel... Mr Quiller is determined to prosecute this business to its fullest extent and so convince Weston that he is not to be trifled with nor have his property taken from him under groundless pretences.'

The Quillers were already in trouble with the law at that time since both William and his father John had been ordered to stand trial in London along with Richard Oliver, charged with possessing contraband. The principal witness for the prosecution was a local man, Robert Coath, who Job did his utmost to discredit. 'If this rascal was not to be silenced he would ruin every smuggler in this place,' he told the Guernsey dealers Nicholas Maingy and Brothers in November 1797, adding that he had arranged for several farmers in the Polperro neighbourhood to testify that Coath was a liar:

'I hope these men will invalidate Coath's evidence and that Messrs Quiller and Oliver will get through this unpleasant business. Should credit be given to Coath's evidence Oliver & Co. would be fined heavy for the goods seized in a cellar - which I hope however they will not.'

Whether Coath, a local agricultural labourer, was induced to give evidence against the Quillers or did so out of revenge is not clear. Whatever the reason, Job went to great lengths to discredit the man's testimony, employing his considerable influence in the process.

In later years, another generation of the ill-fated Quillers met with similar misfortune. Two of the sons of Richard Quiller, also named Richard and John, were lost at sea in an armed merchant ship out of Teneriffe in 1812. But despite the tragedies that afflicted it, the Quiller family remained a formidable influence on Polperro's maritime trading links with Guernsey and elsewhere for many years to come.

7

Captain Gabriel Bray

The ten years between 1783 and 1793 when England was at peace with France and her neighbours saw the smuggling trade at Polperro flourish as never before. Many of those engaged in privateering during the period of conflict were quick to turn their attention to another equally profitable activity.

Polperro's landward isolation made it particularly difficult for the authorities to catch the smugglers in possession of contraband goods. Repeated attempts by Excise officers to do so following a tip-off were more often than not frustrated in spite of the presence of a Customs Officer, Thomas Pinsent, resident there since 1766.

The riding officers appointed to patrol the coast were too few and ill-equipped to carry out the duties demanded of them by their London masters, whose knowledge of Cornwall was often scant. From time to time directives would be circulated to the ports by the Custom House in London, urging greater vigilance in the war against the smugglers:

5th August, 1791
Information having been received that there are now laying in Guernsey upwards of fifty luggers, cutters and tub boats laden with spirits and tobacco which are about to sail for different parts of the English coast between Lands End and the Isle of Wight.
I have it in command to direct you to communicate this matter to all the officers of your port particularly to those of the Water Guard as likewise to the Commanders of such Admiralty cruisers as may be stationed at or in

the neighbourhood and to excite them in the strongest manner to keep a good look out and to use their utmost endeavour to intercept and seize any spirits or tobacco that may be attempted to be clandestinely brought into this kingdom as also all vessels employed in such illicit trade, taking care to appraise the Board of any matter that may arise in consequence.

This concern was shared by Parliament where Pitt, elected Prime Minister with an overwhelming mandate for reform in 1784, began to reduce some of the heaviest duties on imports in the hope of stopping the smugglers' activities. The duty on tea, for instance, was cut from 119% to 12%. He also insisted that the methods employed against smuggling had to be made more effective. Owners of small, fast vessels and large, open boats were required to hold Admiralty licences and a number of well-armed and equipped Revenue cutters were built to patrol the Channel coast.

Early in March 1794, a violent confrontation took place in Polperro between a group of smugglers and Revenue officials that resulted in one of the fishermen being sentenced to death for his part in the affray; only Job's intervention saving his life. The incident followed a dawn raid on Polperro led by the Excise Supervisor from Bodmin, David Llewyn accompanied by two other Revenue officers armed with search warrants and a platoon of fourteen soldiers from the Yorkshire militia. They called first on Thomas Pinsent the local Customs officer, who led them to several cottages including one overlooking the harbour near the pier belonging to Richard Rowett where Llewyn had been given a tip-off that contraband liquor was concealed. Finding the door to the cellar locked, Llewyn ordered one of the soldiers to break in through a window and open it from the inside. There they discovered more than 200 five-gallon casks with rope slings for carrying them still attached. Using a gimlet, the officers broached one and found it contained brandy.

Llewyn ordered his men to remove the casks and take them to Pinsent's house nearby for safekeeping. As they began to do so, however, the sound of gunfire was heard coming from the harbour area where a large crowd had gathered on the quayside opposite the spot where the soldiers were guarding Rowett's cellar. Several of the men were armed with sticks, clubs and muskets; some had even carried a ship's swivel-gun onto the quay while others shouted and swore at the Revenue men and soldiers attempting to move the casks. In a nearby lane more than a hundred Polperro men had assembled and another swivel-gun was drawn up, aimed straight at the cellar door, its touch-hole primed with powder ready to fire, a slow-burning fuse held menacingly by one of the men close by.

One of the Revenue officers ordered some of the soldiers to fix bayonets and advance with him towards the swivel-guns. They were at once surrounded by the crowd, one of whom grabbed the officer's cutlass and threatened to kill him with it if he and his men did not leave the area. Shouts, curses and threats rang out while Pinsent, fearing further violence and even bloodshed, begged Llewyn not to order his soldiers to fire into the crowd. For several tense minutes the two sides confronted one another in the narrow street by the harbour until eventually the Revenue men, aware they were outnumbered and fearing for their safety, abandoned their haul and retreated to the safety of a nearby inn.

Several weeks later, the Revenue officers returned to Polperro with a force of more than one hundred soldiers, intent on arresting several of the men known to have been involved in the affray outside Richard Rowett's cellar. One of those named was John Langmaid a 39-year-old Polperro fisherman who had been positively identified as having threatened Llewyn with a bayonet during the confrontation on the quayside. Although none of the wanted men could be found by the soldiers on this second visit, Langmaid was eventually arrested and charged with unlawful assembly and armed assault on a King's Excise officer.

At John Langmaid's trial at the Old Bailey in London in October 1795, Llewyn testified that Langmaid had approached him brandishing a bayonet in one hand and a musket in the other, threatening 'he would run me through if I did not desist. I thought my life was in danger.' Langmaid was found guilty and, since assaulting a King's Revenue officer was a capital offence, sentenced to death by the court. He would certainly have suffered the same fate as so many other smugglers arrested for similar offences had it not been for Zephaniah Job's intervention.

As soon as news of Langmaid's conviction reached Polperro, his wife Mary at once appealed to Job for help in pleading for her husband's life. Job wrote to John Phillipps Carpenter, a prominent landowner and lawyer whose help he had already sought in connection with the case:

'I'm sorry to trouble you again on this disagreeable business, but at the pressing request of his wife I have to desire the favour of you to speak to the Recorder, Sir John William Rose to report this cause so favourable as possible to the King, as a petition will be sent up by this post on his behalf to His Majesty, signed by several respectable people.'

Job went to considerable lengths on Langmaid's behalf, using his connections to secure the help of other influential figures, including Charles Rashleigh, a prominent lawyer and member of the wealthy landowning Rashleigh family at Menabilly near Fowey. In an extraordinary move, Job persuaded Rashleigh and a small group of influential figures to travel with him to Truro where, over dinner with the High Sheriff of Cornwall, Ralph Allen Daniell*, it was agreed that a petition should be sent to the Duke of Portland, then Home Secretary, seeking a royal pardon for Langmaid. It evidently succeeded, for only a few weeks later, Langmaid was reprieved and ordered instead to serve at sea in the Royal Navy. Convicted smugglers were usually sentenced to at least five years naval or military service if the court decided

---

* Ralph Allen Daniell of Trelissick was one of the principal investors in the mining industry at St. Agnes during the latter part of the 18th century. Known as 'Guinea-a-minute Daniell', he amassed enormous wealth from his investments.

they were fit enough, though many preferred prison where conditions were often easier than life aboard a man-of-war.

Job's delight at the outcome was evident when he wrote afterwards to one of the Guernsey merchants:

'Nothing hath given me so much pleasure that my exertion in favour of John Langmaid hath been crowned with success.'

Not long afterwards, Job wrote again to John Phillipps Carpenter at his home near Tavistock in Devon, offering congratulations on the lawyer's appointment as a Justice of the Peace, adding:

'I sincerely wish more of the independent landed country gentlemen, and less of the clergy, would grace the bench.'

In the same letter, Job mentions that he had spoken to Mr Quiller 'to bring a keg of best cognac, rum and gin which he hath promised to get at first opportunity,' and adding 'I shall also desire my correspondent in Guernsey to send the best that can be had in the island.'

The Carpenters were Westcountry landowners whose estates included the manors of Lansallos and Raphael near Polperro. Job not only acted as steward to the family for an annual salary of six guineas, but supplied them with smuggled liquor as well. It was little wonder magistrates were often reluctant to convict those who appeared before them on smuggling charges!

If the Revenue officers on land were being frustrated in their attempts to put an end to the smuggling trade, the Revenue cutters at sea met with rather more success. One Revenue vessel in particular came to be feared by the Polperro smugglers more than any other. The *Hind*, one of the newest and largest cutters in service, carrying a crew of 41 men, was stationed in the Channel between Portland and Lands End. Like other Revenue cutters in service at the time, the *Hind* was a former smuggling lugger seized off Plymouth in January 1789 and judged too useful to suffer the usual fate and be broken up. Instead, she was converted into a cutter and taken into service. Broad beamed, with little freeboard, her low deck level was compensated for by high red-painted bulwarks into which gunports had been cut. Her sixteen carriage guns on the gun deck were of the new carronade type.* As well as the carriage guns, the *Hind* carried a swivel gun in the stern. The small boats on her deck were used for boarding and patrol work inshore. At sea, with her large gaff mainsail, double square topsails and large jib set, she presented a daunting sight to any Polperro lugger plying between Guernsey and the Cornish coast

Her commander, Lieutenant Gabriel Bray, had served aboard Revenue cutters since 1779 with a zeal and determination that won the admiration of his superiors and gained him a reputation for dealing ruthlessly with smugglers. A few years earlier, while in command of the Revenue cutter *Scourge* off the Kent coast, Bray had confronted a notorious smuggler named Brown in the act of landing spirits on the beach near Deal. The ensuing fight was graphically described in the *Whitehall Evening Post*:

> 'Captain Bray boarded him; and though Brown presented a blunderbuss, both of them not being half a distance from each other, the Captain was not daunted. One of his men seeing his brave master in this situation, with a cutlass cut Brown's cheek clean off. Bray seconded the stroke, and with his cutlass nearly severed his head from his body and put a period to this pirate's life.'

It was not long before Gabriel Bray made his presence felt in Cornwall where the Revenue officials at Fowey were quick to enlist his help in putting an end to the trade so openly carried on in Polperro. In the summer of 1789, he announced his appointment to command the *Hind* by placing a notice in the *Sherborne Mercury* for five successive weeks:

---

* Carronades were very short, light carriage guns that used a small propellant charge to fire a relatively heavy shot for a limited range.

LIEUTENANT GABRIEL BRAY, COMMANDER of the Hind REVENUE SCHOONER, in the service of His Majesty's Customs, now repaired and ready for sea, takes this method of acquainting the public that his station extends from Portland to St Ives Bay and that he is desirous for the good of the revenue to enter into a correspondence with any person or persons who will give him information of goods about to be illegally landed, or where sunk ready for landing; and will, if the said goods are taken by him, give to the person who informed him thereof, one third of his share of seizure money, besides a present over and above out of his own pocket.

Likewise he promises to conceal all such persons who shall give informations, and that they shall never appear in case of law suits in any court. The port he uses chiefly is Fowey, in Cornwall, and should any person residing near there who cannot write wish to give him regular informations, Lieutenant Bray can show such persons a method of corresponding with him just as clear and intelligible as writing, if the person will only wait on Lieutenant Bray at his house in Fowey for a few minutes.

N.B. Correspondents are desired to pay the postage of all letters otherwise no attention will be paid to them.

Hind Schooner, June 15, 1789

Bray's extraordinary promise to share any seizure rewards with his informants would have been a tempting inducement to those who knew of the smugglers' activities, and may well account for some of his early success.

When the *Sedwell*, a big privateer cutter belonging to William Johns whose father had commanded the ill-fated *Swallow* more than a decade earlier, arrived in Polperro in the summer of 1797, Job recorded:

'She had a very narrow escape of being taken by Captain Bray, who took a small boat belonging to Charles Hutton and Co.'

A year later the *Sedwell* was also seized for smuggling and sold by auction at Fowey.

In September 1797, Job reported in a letter to the Guernsey merchants Nicholas Maingy & Co. that Richard Rowett had 144 kegs of spirit 'seized out of a cellar by Captain Bray's men as he came overland'.

Bray led another raid in April the following year after receiving a tip-off that a large number of casks of liquor were about to be landed near Polperro and hidden in the cellar of a local fisherman, William Minards. Knowing that surprise was vital if he was to impound the goods before they were moved, Bray ordered the *Hind*'s second officer, Hugh Pearce, to approach Polperro from the sea with two boatloads of armed crewmen while he made his way overland from Polruan. On the way, Bray called at the rectory at Lansallos to obtain a search warrant from the Reverend Charles Kendall before continuing on the Polperro where he met up with Pearce and the boat party who had already arrived outside Minard's cellar. Leaving the *Hind* crewmen to guard the spot where the kegs were stored, Bray and his second officer went in search of a constable.

Unable to find one, the two men returned to find a large crowd gathering angrily outside the cellar led by Richard Rowett*, his cousin Benjamin Rowett and brother-in-law Reginald Barrett claiming that no Custom House officer had a right to seize anything on shore.

The ensuing scene was reminiscent of Llewyn's earlier attempt to seize contraband goods there. In Bray's absence, some of the mob had entered the cellar and were preparing to carry off the casks inside when two of the *Hind*'s crew, John Hawkins and Richard Verran, attempted to stop them. Verran grabbed a cask from the shoulder of one man but as he did

---

* Richard Rowett (1770-1848) was the eldest son of Richard and Ann Rowett of Polperro and later commander of the privateer Unity. Like the Quillers, the Rowetts featured prominently in the smuggling and privateering activities there.

so, both he and Hawkins were set upon and manhandled out of the cellar by the crowd, now rapidly swelling in number as news of the raid spread through Polperro. Outside, Hugh Pearce found himself thrust up against the wall of the building by Richard Rowett who grabbed him by the collar and threatened to beat his brains out. At the same time, Benjamin Rowett warned he would shoot the first man to lay a hand on the cellar door while his fellow smugglers removed the kegs inside. When eventually Gabriel Bray and his crew did succeed in entering the cellar with the aid of a detachment of Lancashire Militia, they found most of the kegs had been removed or destroyed.

Infuriated at being thwarted yet again, Gabriel Bray determined that the ringleaders should be brought to justice for their part in the affray. Warrants were issued for the arrest of four Polperro men who had been positively identified as having prevented the Revenue officers from seizing the goods: the two Rowett cousins, Richard and Benjamin, together with Reginald Barrett and John Minards, son of the owner of the cellar where the liquor had been stored.

Although charges of armed assault and obstruction against all four were read out at a court hearing at Westminster in June 1799, the case was never proceeded with.

Had Job intervened yet again on behalf of the Polperro smugglers? If so, it was one of the last occasions when he was able to use his influence to prevent justice from taking its course.

Gabriel Bray, determined to put a stop to the smuggling trade at Polperro, was soon to take a decisive role in the Revenue service's efforts to suppress it.

8

Revolutionary War

Across the Channel in 1793, the streets of Paris echoed to the rumble of tumbrils and the thud of the guillotine as another year of the bloody Reign of Terror in France began. Little more than a week after Louis XV and most of his family were executed on January 21st before a crowd of 20,000 spectators in the Place de la Revolution, the National Convention of Paris declared war on Great Britain.

In England there was an immediate embargo on trade with France and merchant vessels were permitted to carry arms. Polperro greeted the news with joy. Ten years had passed since privateering had last been possible and the Quillers in particular wasted no time in buying and fitting out a large sloop built the previous year at Mevagissey named the *Lively*. Once again, Job undertook the task of book-keeping for the venture, devoting several more pages of his ledger for the purpose. This time he debited the Guernsey merchant Nicholas Maingy, one of the main sources of smuggled goods, with nearly £200 for a quarter share of the cost of fitting out the *Lively* for her first cruise in June under the command of Richard Quiller.

Within a few days of putting to sea, the *Lively* had the good fortune to be present when *HMS Crescent* captured a French merchant vessel, *Le Club de Cherbourg*. In accordance with privateering custom the prize court ruled that the *Lively* was entitled to a share of the proceeds, a decision that would have been resented by the Navy who regarded privateers as little more than undisciplined smugglers.

A month later, the *Lively* took another French prize, *La Jeune Eulalie* which Job then sold to the Maingy brothers in Guernsey for £510. Tragedy struck the unfortunate Quiller family soon afterwards when the *Lively's* commander, Richard Quiller, was lost at sea leaving Job with the difficulty of sharing out the proceeds of both prizes among her crew. More than three years later Job wrote to the Guernsey dealers, Nicholas Maingy, explaining that he had been unable to distribute any of the prize money to the crew because Richard Quiller had kept the only list of those aboard the *Lively* at the time of the prize captures 'and out of delicacy to his widow his father hath not yet examined his papers and thereby left all their accounts unsettled.'

Richard's father, John, had meanwhile commanded another successful Polperro privateer, the *Brilliant*, whose capture of a large Spanish ship netted a substantial portion of the £8,800 prize money for Job and the Quiller family. And the *Sedwell*, in which Job and the Maingy brothers also had a share, captured the French privateer *La Ami Planteur*.

Job's involvement in this privateering venture during the early months of the Revolutionary War with France in 1793 earned him a substantial share of the proceeds. For a while, the contraband trade declined. Revenue vessels had inflicted huge losses on the Polperro smugglers during the two previous years of peace, when more than a dozen boats had been seized on their return from Guernsey.

The outbreak of war also led to further increases in taxes on a wide range of goods such as tobacco, brandy and gin. Even salt eventually attracted a tax of 15 shillings a bushel, thirty or forty times what it cost, and an extortionate amount to men and women earning a shilling a day who depended on salt for preserving fish and pig meat for the winter. Some Polperro fishermen were unable even to earn enough to buy salt to preserve pilchards for their own families and as a result the fish were dumped as manure on the fields. The pilchard fishing industry, already badly hit by the loss of its markets overseas because of the war, suffered badly.

Revenue cutters in the Channel took an active part in the war at sea without relaxing their campaign against the smugglers. Early in 1793, letters of marque were granted to Gabriel Bray in command of the *Hind*, authorising him to seize French shipping but in view of his determination to suppress the smuggling trade in Polperro it is unlikely that Bray devoted much time to the French. Only a few weeks later, the *Hind* was active in recapturing a Polperro boat, the *Assistance*, which had escaped the custody of another Revenue vessel. As the war continued, so did the losses suffered by the smugglers. In due course, Britain's allies against the French were either defeated or dropped out of the struggle and by 1797, Britain faced France alone. It was a time of invasion scares and food shortages. Press gangs repeatedly raided coastal towns and merchant shipping in order to overcome the Navy's desperate shortage of seamen. And taxes were again increased to pay for the war effort, adding further incentive to the smugglers.

France did little to discourage the traffic in contraband goods across the Channel since the smugglers were often the unwitting source of useful intelligence during the war years. They also suffered losses at the hands of French privateers. When the crew of a Polperro smuggling boat were captured by a French vessel in 1797, Job wrote on behalf of the owners to the Maingy brothers requesting a discount on the lost cargo:

'These goods were sold at the ready money price and were to be paid for in full, lost or not lost. They admitted it, but said it was such a very unfortunate affair their being taken by the French, and the expense they have been at to procure their men which were impressed before when captured by the Revenue cruiser, they thought you would not object to make them some allowance and in such case they would pay their bill at once.'

The owners of this particular vessel had, it seems, been doubly unfortunate for the crew had been captured by both Revenue and French boats in turn.

More than two dozen Polperro men were languishing in French prisons in 1811, by which time Britain had been at war with France for 17 years, interrupted only by the brief Peace of . A public subscription was held in Cornwall that year for the relief of Cornish prisoners of war then incarcerated at the various French detention centres. The amount eventually received by each prisoner was £2..5s..11d. When the list of the recipients was published by Lord Falmouth, who had been actively associated with the promotion of the scheme, eleven Polperro men's names appeared among those held at Cambrai in Normandy, while a further 15 were being held in the depot at Sarre Libre.

Many other Polperro mariners had been released earlier and others had died in captivity, having endured the hardships and tedium of prison life, all victims of desperate but unavailing encounters with French warships and privateers at sea.

When news reached Polperro in October 1801 that a treaty was about to be signed between Britain, France, Spain and Holland that would bring an end to hostilities, an extraordinary event took place there. To celebrate the prospect of peace local people organised an illumination, every cottage and building displaying lights in their windows after darkness fell so that the entire harbour area and surrounding hillside was lit up. The following night, a great bonfire was lit on Chapel Hill overlooking the village and everyone gathered round it with much shouting and firing of guns to signal the forthcoming ceasefire. Afterwards, Job and the other principal inhabitants made their way to the Ship Inn in Fore Street where the landlord, Charles Guy, had prepared a grand festive supper for them during which, according to one contemporary report, 'a variety of sentimental toasts, some with excellent loyal songs, closed the festivity of the night.'

Such joy in Polperro at the prospect of peace seems odd considering the extent to which the local economy thrived during the wars with France. Inevitably, when the Peace of Amiens was eventually declared the following year, privateering was halted and the armed smuggling vessels that roamed the Channel began to prove a particular source of embarrassment to the authorities. The truce that followed lasted little more than twelve months before Britain was once again at war with France, when the Emperor Napoleon Bonaparte threatened to invade England.

Job at once set about organising another privateering venture, this time with William Johns, the 35-year-old commander of the *Industry*, a fine single-masted, square-sterned cutter built at Fowey the previous year. Armed with ten guns and carrying a crew of 36 men equipped with small arms, cutlasses and enough provisions for three months at sea, the *Industry* presented a formidable threat to any enemy vessel of similar size.

Before setting out, however, the *Industry* required the necessary letters of marque. Job instructed his London agents, Brock & Lemesurier in Throgmorton Street, to apply for commissions against French and Dutch vessels since Holland was under French occupation at the time. Irving Brock duly attended the Admiralty Court himself on June 20th 1803 in Doctors' Commons near St Paul's cathedral on behalf of William Johns declaring that Zephaniah Job was the sole owner of the *Industry*.

'That the said *William Johns'* Ship is called the *Industry* belonging to the *Port of Looe in Cornwall*, is of the Burthen of *about eighty five* Tons, *is a square sterned clinker Cutter fitted as a sloop with a plain head and* has *one Mast*, that the said *William Johns* goeth Commander of her, that she is mounted with six Carriage Guns, carrying Shot of *1, 1/2, & 2* Pounds Weight, and *four* Swivel Guns, is navigated with *thirty six* Men, of whom One-Third are Landmen, has *twenty* Small Arms, *thirty* Cutlasses, *twenty* Barrels of Powder, *fifty* Rounds of Great Shot, and about *two hundred* Weight of Small Shot, that the said Ship is victualled for *three* Months, has *three* Suits of Sails, *three* Anchors, *three* Cables, and about *five hundred* Weight of Spare Cordage, that *James Ellis* goeth Mate or Lieutenant, *George Rose* Gunner, *William Pitt* Boatswain, *John*

Canning Carpenter, *Henry Addington* Cook, and *William Windham* Surgeon of the said Ship and that *Zephaniah Job of the Parish of Talland in the Country of Cornwall is the sole* Owner and Setter-out of the said Ship.'

An entry in Job's ledger at the time suggests that an objection to the application had been lodged by the Customs, who probably suspected the *Industry* would engage in smuggling as well as privateering. In the event, letters of marque were granted at a cost of £22..14s each and the *Industry* was soon on her way in pursuit of foe.

Nelson's victory at Trafalgar in 1805 followed, providing yet another excuse for celebration at Polperro as elsewhere. Privateering there continued to prosper. Two of the most successful vessels engaged against the French were the *Unity,* commanded by Richard Rowett and the *Pheasant,* by William Quiller. The *Pheasant* was a schooner, considered at the time to be a modern rig, but better adapted for coastal sailing than the old square-sailed brigs and much easier to manoeuvre during a fight.

Napoleon's eventual defeat at Waterloo in June 1815 brought the wars with France finally to an end. Word reached Polperro a few days later when Sir Harry Trelawny's daughter, Mary Harding recorded in her diary 'the fine news of Bonaparte's entire defeat by Lord Wellington, never was there heard of so glorious a battle.' The following month hundreds of people gathered in Plymouth Sound in boats to catch sight of the defeated Napoleon standing at the quarter rail of *HMS Bellerophon* a few hours before his departure for St. Helena.

9

Man of Business

Although he became known as the 'Smugglers' Banker', Zephaniah Job not only acted as agent and banker for smugglers and privateers, but merchant, general man of business and steward to an unrivalled extent in the neighbourhood of Polperro at the beginning of the 19th century.

Over a period of some forty years, he bought and sold corn, shipped grain, sold lime and ashes to farmers, owned lime kilns and barges, exported pilchards, and bought bricks, coal and linen into Polperro as well as being steward, farmer and timber merchant. In addition, Job drafted leases, made wills and wrote letters on behalf of his many clients.

As early as 1778 Job, then just 29 years of age, had established himself as an agent for two of the Guernsey merchants who supplied the Polperro smugglers, Jean Guille & Co. and Messrs Jersey & De Lisle. It is probable that he had by then abandoned his role as schoolmaster for the pages of his earliest ledger, begun in 1778, are filled with entries recording payments for goods shipped from Guernsey while subsequent entries relate to the Polperro privateers *Swallow, Good Intent* and the *Brilliant*. Other pages are devoted to his stewardships for Sir Harry Trelawny, the Reverend Benjamin Shipman, rector of Lansallos, and his curate, the Reverend Thomas Donnithorne. There is even an account for his elder brother, John Job, against which the following entry appears:

1779, August 17. Settled account with brother John Job for the rent of Mingoes Coomb tenement.

This is the first indication that Job renewed contact with his family in St. Agnes after arriving at Polperro. 'Mingoes Coomb' is an area known today as Mingoose coombe on the opposite side of St. Agnes Beacon to the Polberro mine where Zephaniah Job probably underwent his mining education before fleeing as a penniless fugitive barely a decade or so earlier. Now he was in a position to help his family and subsequent entries over a ten year period reveal that he paid out more than £82 in rent, loans and interest payments on behalf of his brother John.

Almost as early are Job's sales of lime and ashes to local farmers from the lime kilns at Shallowpool a mile or so up the West Looe river. In 1785, he entered into a partnership with John Grigg and Son, corn merchants at Looe, that prospered for many years and expanded into a wide range of activities. Cargoes of barley and oats were shipped to buyers in Guernsey and Liverpool. Limestone was shipped from the Plymouth quarries as ballast or cargo to be burned in the kilns at Looe, Polperro and at Lerryn on the River Fowey where it was converted into powdered lime, for lime, seaweed, sand, waste pilchards and spent salt were in great demand as fertilisers by the local farmers.

The Polperro lime kilns on the harbour produced 7,450 bushels of lime in 1796 at 18 pence a bushel for small quantities; anyone buying large amounts had a reduction and paid 14 pence a bushel. The kilns were also used for corn drying and there are many entries by Job of payments to women loading corn into boats as well as carrying it to the kilns. The lime kilns were eventually bought by Job when the Raphael manor estate was sold.

Job's trading partnership with John Grigg and Son thrived on the buying and selling of oats, barley and wheat and lasted until the turn of the century, Robert Grigg taking over after the death of his father in 1794. The trade included clover seeds, and much of the grain shipped from Looe to buyers in other parts of Britain was carried by Job's schooner, the *Polperro*, from 1805 when it was commanded by John Clements.

Job continued trading in grain right up until the last years of his life. As late as December 1818, dealing with a firm of corn merchants at Emsworth, near Portsmouth, he wrote saying he had been waiting to see what the grain prices were at Liskeard fair before adding: 'I have shipped two cargoes for Bristol lately.'

The trade was fraught with risk, even for someone as experienced as Job. The same month he was offering to ship a cargo of grain to the Hampshire merchants, a local customer, William Crees, cancelled an order he had placed earlier. Job's angry response, was swift and to the point:

'I have much greater reason than you can possibly have to be displeased with your letter to me refusing to take the wheat and barley which you ordered me to purchase for you. I do most solemnly declare (and my word hath always been accepted by my respectable friends) and I have offered you my oath that when you gave me an order to purchase barley for you on the road from Looe, you ordered me to purchase wheat. In consequence I put off all my other correspondents and dealers and now that the price of corn is fallen I am to have it left on my hands to look out for new dealers when I can find them. I think you will have difficulty to reconcile this to your own feelings...'

Job's method of dealing with defaulters, no doubt perfected over many years of persuading reluctant smugglers to pay for goods supplied, was forthright and emphatic. Replying to another recalcitrant customer in 1819, he wrote:

'Is it possible for you to write to me in this manner? I have often told you, and now repeat it, that if you will come forward with your accounts and settle them with me honestly and fairly there is nothing that you could reasonably require of me but that I would do for you. But after a lapse of nearly two years to be told that you will render me no account nor pay me for the corn is monstrous.'

Despite such difficulties, the corn trade occupied as much of Job's business dealings as any other, and was certainly continued over a longer period than most. As with the timber and lime trade, he began in partnership with others who provided the initial capital until he was eventually able to finance the business himself.

Although fishing was the principal industry of Polperro it was only after the introduction of seine fishing there by 1782 that a thriving export trade in pilchards with Italy began to develop in which Job played a significant role. In seine fishing, a large net was used to enclose a shoal of pilchards; larger and larger nets were used as time went by in order that whole shoals could be caught at one time so that the catches were often of such quantity that made exporting worthwhile. 1790 saw one of the best pilchard fishing seasons ever, and throughout the period of the French Revolutionary and Napoleonic wars the pilchards were plentiful in most years, although the export market for Polperro fish in Italy was closed for several years because of the conflict. In 1795, despite noting 'we have still on this coast a very gloomy prospect in the pilchard fishery,' Job shipped 450 hogsheads of pilchards, more than a million fish, to the Italian port of Leghorn near Pisa aboard the brig *Richard and Mary*. The war with France meant that such a voyage via the Straits of Gibralter was a risky undertaking for any merchant vessel and required a naval escort. Not surprisingly, the insurance premium on such a cargo was more than ten times higher than normal; the *Richard and Mary* and cargo was insured for £1,500 for the voyage to Italy, though Job received a repayment of £46..16s on the premium because the vessel had fallen in with a naval convoy for most of the journey. Despite its safe arrival, Job told the Leghorn merchants:

'I fear we shall see very little profit by the cargo as the freight and insurance are so very high.'

The pilchard catches the following year surpassed all expectations. Job acted swiftly, buying another 650 hogsheads of fish and shipping them aboard the *Dispatch* brig for the three week voyage to Leghorn. Because of the risks involved, the trade was short-lived, and in later years the Italians established two fish processing factories on the quayside in Polperro.

Barges brought coal to Polperro as well as the anthracite dust from Wales for use in the lime kilns. Linen arrived by sea from Ireland. Timber from the neighbouring woodlands was shipped out and the sea-going traffic in and out of the harbour was never busier. The harbour itself belonged to the Carpenter and Phillipps families until the sale of Raphael Manor in 1811, when it was bought by Job. He collected the harbour dues from the fishermen and, when the Preventive boat was moored there, from the Customs Collector at Looe, as he did the rent from the tenants of the various farms in the area.

From the parlour adjoining his cottage in Polperro, Job worked every day of the year and, as his neatly copied letter-books reveal, his quill pen was not even laid down on Christmas Day in 1786. Every letter he wrote was carefully copied by hand either by himself or one of his clerks, sometimes even by his young nephew Zephaniah Job who came to work for his uncle in Polperro for a time.

Zephaniah Job Junior, as he always signed his name on documents and correspondence in connection with his uncle's business, was the eldest son of Job's brother, John, a victualling merchant in St. Agnes. Because he had no family of his own, Job planned one day to hand over his business affairs to his nephew, but the young Zephaniah's relationship with his uncle was marred by his excessive drinking and gambling habits, so much so that by March 1797 Job wrote to a family friend about the 'unparalleled ingratitude of my nephew':

'His conduct of late hath become so notorious to every respectable friend of mine and to every person and place he hath lately visited as to excite their astonishment, and having almost entirely given himself over to gaming and drunkeness I much fear he is irreversibly lost... I have shown him that if he behaved well no one had a fairer prospect to make themselves respected and respectable in the world, but on the contrary if he behaved improperly no one had a worse prospect than himself. A few weeks ago on remonstrating with him strongly on the impropriety of his conduct he acknowledged himself in fault and promised to leave off drinking and attend to business in future when I forgave him all his past misconduct but had the mortification to find his resolutions were very superficial and that he presently fell into greater enormities of gaming and drunkeness than before. I cannot put into words the degree to which my feelings hath been harrowed up for near two years last past by my nephew's inattention and ingratitude to me and by a sense of his plunging himself into inevitable ruin.'

Job's 23-year-old nephew parted company from his uncle and Polperro soon afterwards. There are one or two later entries in Job's account books for occasional payments to him: 1805 'advanced my nephew Zephaniah £5' and again in the same year there is an entry of £6 'for my nephew Zephaniah'. What became of his wayward namesake is not recorded, although he certainly did not live long enough to benefit from his uncle's estate.

Because of the enormous number of letters he sent and received each year, Job's outlay in postage expences amounted to more than £100 a year, much of which he recovered from his various clients. When, in 1796, the mail coach that travelled regularly between Looe and Fowey, stopping to leave any items of post for Polperro at the crossroads known as Barcelona near Trelawne, was discontinued, Job wrote to the General Post Office headquarters in London protesting at the effect such a move was having on businesses in the area. For a while he was obliged to send one his servants on horse into Looe and Fowey every day to collect any letters for him but, in due course, a regular wagon link between Polperro and Looe was established, largely as a result of Job's endeavours.

In addition to his many other business activities, Job undertook a great deal of work that would today be done by a solicitor. As well as acting as executor to many Polperro families, he also drafted leases, conveyances and other legal documents. At the time, the art of conveyancing was a complicated mystery to most people and such dealings with land or family settlement usually involved great expense and difficulty. In 1804 he was admitted as a member of the Middle Temple in London as a licenced conveyancer. And when, a few years later in 1819, there was an attempt to introduce a bill in Parliament reforming the practice of conveyancing, Job wrote to the two MPs for Fowey, Glynn Campbell and Lord Valletort, reminding them of his support when they had stood for election the previous year and adding:

'I have been a Conveyancer upwards of forty years and no instrument drawn or prepared by me hath ever been found illegal or defective, and having devoted my time to the study and practice of conveyancing, and have on that account given up other pursuits in life, I am convinced you will see with me the injustice of being deprived of carrying on my lawful business in case the intended bill is to have a retrospective operation.'

Job was by now 70 years old, and it seems remarkable he should have gone to such lengths to oppose the bill. Yet it was perhaps entirely characteristic of him that he should want to continue practicing what he had spent a considerable part of his life in Polperro doing, right up until his death a little over two years later.

10

Smugglers' Banker

Zephaniah Job's role as the Polperro smugglers' banker originated with his stewardship to Sir Harry Trelawny. When, on the 5th of January 1789, the baronet, by then £1,510 in debt to his steward, gave Job a note of hand for £1,000 it marked the effective beginning of Job's function as a banker.

At the time, little more than two years after an account had been opened in the name of the Reverend Sir Harry Trelawny on the first page of the thick walnut-brown crown folio ledger Job kept at his cottage, both men were content to let the debt stand. A year later, Job debited Sir Harry's account £45 for twelve months interest on the note at four and a half per cent interest. The account remained in debit for the next 17 years until Sir Harry directed Job to arrange for the sale of the Bochym estate to his son William Lewis, then still at Oxford University, thus transferring the deficit to another member of the family. By the end of 1816, the Trelawny family still owed Job at least £4,000.

Job also managed the finances of the Eastcotts, another genteel family in the neighbourhood. Richard Eastcott had been the rector of Lansallos until his death in 1779, when his widow Susanna moved to Lostwithiel. When she died in December 1786, Job paid all the funeral expenses and during subsequent years paid the school and clothing accounts for the three Eastcott children, drawing a salary of five guineas a year for his work. Throughout this period their account was in debit with Job until it was finally carried forward to Mrs Eastcott's son, Thomas, who later became a captain in the Royal Cornwall Militia. Unlike his two less fortunate sisters, who had to manage on rentals of between £50 and £60 each, Thomas Sandford Eastcott enjoyed a large income of more than £1,000 a year at the age of 25 in 1795, and in due course his debt to Job was cleared.

Fortunately for Job, not all his clients required him to finance them for nearly twenty years as the Trelawny and the Eastcott families did. Although he also acted as steward and banker to the Carpenter family, who owned Raphael manor, the joint account he kept for Sir Jonathan Phillipps and John Phillipps Carpenter was invariably debited with small payments for smuggled brandy, tea, coffee, snuff and linen supplied by Job as, for example, in December 1794:

> To Carteret Priaulx of Guernsey
> for 2lbs of Strasbourg Snuff at 1/-   2s..0d
> To do. for 50lbs of Coffee at 13d   £2..14..2d
> To do. for a piece of fine Cambrick   £4..13..6d
> To do. for 12lbs Hyson tea at 5/6d   £3.. 6..0d

Job's method of charging interest to those whose accounts were in debit was based on the principle of simple interest, charged on the amount owing at the beginning of each year regardless of whether it had increased or decreased meanwhile, in contrast to present day banking practice when compound interest is charged. Sometimes he allowed interest to remain unpaid for several years, adding a lump sum only when the account was finally cleared.

When John Quiller the notorious smuggler whose privateering exploits had reaped such rich rewards in prize money, lent Sir Harry Trelawny £1,300 on the joint bond of Job and himself, Job entered the following note in his ledger:

> Sir Harry Trelawny Bart. gave his joint bond with me for the balance of this account (say for £1,300) which is placed to his credit in my account and the balance £51.8.7d is paid Mr Quiller this day - the 24th August, 1800
>   Witness our hand   Z. Job

The payment to Quiller was equivalent to four per cent interest on the original amount. Unlike many who profited from smuggling and privateering only to recklessly squander their gains, John Quiller was a great deal more thrifty and astute, taking full advantage of Job's connections with the Trelawny family. Yet it is inconceivable that Sir Harry was unaware of the origin of his loan, or the nature of the business carried on by the Quillers.

When it came to dealing with the Guernsey merchants who supplied the smugglers, however, an altogether different rate of interest was charged by Job for acting as the banker for such transactions, collecting and forwarding the payments. At first, he added only half of one per cent on the money paid in to their credit by the Polperro smugglers; by 1782, he had increased this to one per cent, adding only the cost of postage. Although small sums of money were often sent in cash across by boat to the Guernsey firms, a substantial proportion was transferred through various London banking houses and agents with whom Job had accounts often running to several thousands of pounds at a time. The scale of these dealings was such that there would have been few in financial circles in London at the time who had not heard of the little fishing port in Cornwall.

In the early days, Job dealt with William De Jersey the London agent who acted for him on behalf of the Polperro privateers, applying for letters of marque, arranging for the legal condemnation of their prizes, paying the proctors' fees as well as remitting money to Guernsey. De Jersey died suddenly in 1784 while Job was still endeavouring to settle the claims arising from the seizure of the *Swallow*'s prize, the *Rusee*, by the *Harlequin*, he employed other agents including Perchard & Brock (later Brock & Lemesurier) and Commerell Lubbock & Co.

In October 1795, Job wrote to two London bankers, Pybus Call & Co. in Old Bond Street and Sir James Esdaile & Co. in Lombard Street:

'Having enlarged my business, I find it will be convenient for me to open an account with a banking house in London. Be pleased to favour me with your terms of transacting business. For any enquiry you may think proper to make, I beg to have to refer you to my nearest neighbours, Sir Harry Trelawny Bart. or Thomas Sandford Eastcott of Port Looe Esqr. either of whom will guarantee any transaction which I may have to do with your house'

To each letter, he added a postscript: 'I may probably draw for about £12,000 or £15,000 per annum.'

Even more remarkable than the anticipated amount of drawings on each account is the fact that Job gave as references the names of the two people most indebted to him at the time; explaining, perhaps, why it was that he allowed such respectable figures to have large debts outstanding with him for so long.

On more than one occasion Job displayed an uncanny instinct for financial opportunism. When, for example, in 1796 Lady Trelawny received news that her eldest son John, serving with the Royal Navy aboard *HMS Dictator* in the West Indies, had been promoted to Lieutenant she confided to Job he was also expecting to share in prize money totalling £30,000 following the capture of an enemy vessel by his ship. Job, ever anxious to expand his list of clients, wrote congratulating the 16-year-old naval officer on his promotion and offering his services:

'My agents in London will give me every assistance that may be wanted there; by this means you will be sure to have your property in safe hands, and I will reserve it for you or plan it out to the best advantage until you return to England. Should you approve of my proposal (which is made entirely with a view to be of service to you) it will be proper for you to send me will and power to receive such prize money and other monies as may be due to you.'

Since there is no account in John Trelawny's name among the many listed by Job, it is unlikely the young Lieutenant took up the offer. His younger brother, William Lewis, did engage Job as his steward and in 1799, when the young Trelawny left Westminster School to go to Oxford, Sir Harry wrote to Job instructing him to open a separate account for his son while at university.

Although Job became known as the smugglers' banker, most of the smugglers did not in fact bank with him. His role was to receive their payments on account of the Guernsey dealers and to remit these, so that he was more of a banker to the Guernsey traders than to the smugglers who were given several months credit from the time the goods were shipped until payment for them was due.

Collecting the money was not always a simple matter. Early in 1788, Job informed Jersey & De Lisle on Guernsey that Thomas Rowett, one of the Polperro smugglers they had supplied goods to, was a 'ruined man.'

'No man has been more unfortunate. Five or six vessels in which he had goods and held a share have been taken successively, which altogether puts it out of his power to pay a shilling at least for the present. These uncommon losses it was impossible to foresee and the man is really emaciated considerably with the reflection of his situation.'

A few months later, Job again reported to the same dealers:

'I shall at once apply for the few debts to your house and hope to receive the greater part thereof shortly. It is all safe except Thomas Rowett who is wretchedly poor, but I believe honest if it may be ever in his power to pay.'

The extent to which the Guernsey suppliers relied on Job to indicate who they could safely supply goods to was an essential part of the trust on which their dealings with the

Polperro smugglers was based. For Job, knowing just who he should safely recommend was often as difficult as collecting the money itself and more than once he was forced to admit:

'I don't know who to recommend, for those who are fair and honest while they have good success too often make shifts and are unwilling to pay when they met with losses.'

As the seizure of vessels by Revenue cutters increased and the determined efforts of the authorities to put an end to smuggling began to take effect, so the hardship in Polperro mounted. 1805 not only saw the introduction of further anti-smuggling legislation, thus further reducing the supply of goods from Guernsey, but the bankruptcy of William Braddon whose shop was one of the principal businesses in Polperro.

Braddon had been one of Job's clients for a number of years; indeed, he had only just been paid by Job for providing the arrangements for John Quiller's funeral a few months before his business failed. After news of Braddon's bankruptcy was announced in the *Exeter Flying Post* in March 1805, Job acted as receiver, ensuring that all creditors (of whom he was one) received at least one third of what they were owed.

Job's continued to act as a financial and insurance agent in Polperro to the extent that he was, to all intent and purpose, operating as a banker. He loaned money at interest and received money on deposit.

Such transactions were invariably accompanied by a promissory note of some sort, not unlike the note of hand Job obtained from Sir Harry Trelawny in 1788 and, since a bank-note was simply a printed promise by the bank issuing it to pay the bearer, on demand, a sum of money, it seemed quite natural to Job that he should eventually begin issuing his own notes for fixed sums of money. Early in 1806, having obtained a banking licence for £20, he asked a London printer to prepare engraving plates for bank-notes of £1, £2 and £5 denominations payable by Christopher Smith Son & Co. one of the London merchant bankers with whom he dealt.

Christopher Smith was an Alderman and Sheriff of the City of London who unsuccessfully contested the parliamentary seat for East Looe in 1806, but later became MP for St Albans and Lord Mayor of London in 1817. His association with Job continued for many years, the two men frequently exchanging gifts; in 1819, Job wrote to the Alderman offering to provide 'a bottle of the best for you should you honour me with a visit at my humble cottage.'

The Polperro bank notes issued by Job were among the first to be circulated in Cornwall, but he was always careful to observe the essential condition of having sufficient coin available in exchange for his paper money. The custom of issuing paper money had originated during the wars with France when the enormous cost of the military effort drastically reduced the amount of gold and silver coinage in circulation. Bank of England notes were declared legal tender and occasionally Job found his creditors preferring them to his own, as in 1819 when he was obliged to exchange six Bank of England £1 notes for his own, observing:

'I have the satisfaction to know that my notes are readily received by every banker in the country and by every respectable merchant and shopkeeper.'

When, only a few years later, he was to die unexpectedly there was still more than enough cash, bonds, bank notes and other funds due to him on all the promissory notes on his bank then in circulation to be honoured.

11

Guernsey Merchants

The bustling town and harbour of St. Peter Port was the key to Guernsey's prosperity during the latter half of the 18th century. Its freedom from import duties, deep anchorage sheltered by the neighbouring islands and entrance guarded by the heavily fortified Castle Cornet, made it the best haven in the Channel Islands. It was here during the wars between Britain and France that the Guernsey merchants grew rich on the profits of privateering and the smuggling trade with England.

Exempt from taxation imposed by a British parliament, it became the single most important centre for the supply of a wide range of contraband goods into Britain during the 18th and 19th centuries. The annual revenue from smuggling or 'Free Trade' as the islanders preferred to call it exceeded £40,000 at its height, more than the total value of Guernsey's legitimate exports to England in the course of a year. Guernsey traders at St. Peter Port imported large quantities of wines and spirits, almost of all for sale to English wholesalers and smugglers. The wine and brandy stored in vaults in the town matured very well in Guernsey's mild climate and this, together with the island's strategic position between France and Britain, combined to make it one of the chief entrepôts of smuggling.

So great was the 'trade' that a secondary industry grew up around it, the manufacture of casks; small, easily carried kegs of ten gallons. By the time British anti-smuggling legislation had been extended to the Channel Islands in 1805, and a Custom House set up in St. Peter Port, there were at least 600 coopers engaged in making them. The vaults and stores in the town were overflowing and some cargoes were even hidden under temporary coverings in the surrounding fields above.

It was thanks to privateering and smuggling, together with shipbuilding and coopering, that some island families made great fortunes, while many others enjoyed considerable wealth for the first time.

Although Job's first dealings were with Jean Guille & Co. of St Peter Port in 1778, most of the business he conducted for nearly 30 years on behalf of the Polperro smugglers was with the four principal Guernsey merchant houses of Jersey & De Lisle (later Peter De Lisle & Sons), Nicholas Maingy & Brothers, John Lukis and Carteret Priaulx. Between 1787 and 1805, he had accounts with at least eight suppliers on the island who, with the exception of Carteret Priaulx & Co., dealt almost exclusively with him when supplying Polperro.

The smugglers usually obtained their supplies from Guernsey on credit terms extending over several months, allowing them time to sell the goods. Job then collected payments from them, acting as guarantor, and forwarded the money to Guernsey, either directly or through one of his London agents. A discount of ten per cent was often allowed for ready money - cash on delivery - as an added incentive for prompt payment.

Job's accounts for the period between 1788 and 1804 give some indication of the scale of the trade with Polperro. The sums he collected on behalf of just three of the Guernsey firms during that period amounted to nearly £100,000: £30,500 credited to Jersey & De Lisle between 1778-1789; a total of £23,000 to Carteret Priaulx between 1778-1799, and an astonishing £42,755 to the Maingy brothers. On average, the Polperro smugglers paid Job a total of nearly £6,000 a year over a twenty year period.

The St Peter Port merchants relied on his recommendation when dealing with the smugglers and he in turn would reassure them that those he represented were dependable, as in 1786:

'I shall be very particular not to take any orders but from honest and safe hands...'

On another occasion, he urged caution:

'People in your line ought to be very careful who they give credit to in these precarious times. Though the people of this place have always paid their merchants for their goods, I know of no one that now comes to your island (hired men excepted) that are safe to deal with.'

The following year Job recommended a new customer:

'Please also supply John Toms with such goods as he may want, and desire you will supply him on the very lowest terms as he is a good dealer and always pays his bills quickly.'

Shipping the goods across to Polperro meant running the gauntlet of the Revenue vessels patrolling the Channel. In the ten years between 1791 and 1801 when the Revenue cutters, including the *Hind* commanded by Gabriel Bray were at their most active off the Cornish coast, more than 30 Polperro vessels were seized and their cargoes impounded. Such losses often made it difficult for Job to pay for goods lost in this way, despite the fact that all orders accepted by him were on the understanding that a discount of only ten per cent was usually allowed.

The long daylight hours during the summer months were particularly hazardous for Polperro smuggling vessels crossing to and from Guernsey. Early in June 1795, Job reported to Carteret Priaulx that the *Happy Return*, owned by Richard Rowett, had been seized after a 28 hour chase at sea, and another boat belonging to John Clemence had also been taken by the Revenue cutter *Spider*.

> 'The risk is now very great for those small craft. I would advise them to do very little during the summer months and while there is such a look out.'

Just two weeks later, he again reported that a further three boats had been seized off the Cornish coast. Since one of them had been outside the limits of the Hovering Act, designed to curb the activities of smuggling vessels operating inshore, a fact witnessed by the captain of a fishing smack who was prepared to testify, Job suggested that Carteret Priaulx pay half the legal costs of contesting the seizure:

> 'There cannot be any doubt recovering the vessel and cargo by calling the captain of the smack to certify the distance they were at the time they were taken. I should think it best for you to assist them to get the ship and cargo restored.'

If the Guernsey merchants were prepared to help finance the smugglers in their legal battles against the Revenue, then they knew too that they could also depend on Job's discretion in his dealings with them. The following year he informed John Lukis, one of the St. Peter Port suppliers:

> 'I have no doubt of selling some cargoes on the terms you mention for ready money, and you may rely on my secrecy. I have just mentioned to one or two particular persons that I can procure them a cargo or two of goods at the current price at the time of shipping it, to allow 10 per cent for ready money and no abatement for loss; but have mentioned no name nor will I until the bargain is made and then I will bind to secrecy.'

The extraordinary lengths Job was prepared to go to on behalf of his smuggling clients is revealed in another letter to Lukis in 1795 following a dispute with one of them over payment for goods:

'From my intimate connection with the magistrates in this neighbourhood I have prevailed on them not to grant search warrants and often saved them heavy fines when they have been prosecuted in the Exchequer. I should not have mentioned this but to show their ingratitude in mentioning my name to you in the manner they did.'

On this occasion, Job sent a signed undertaking from the owners of each of the three vessels involved in the disputed debt to John Lukis in Guernsey, carefully keeping copies himself. One of those involved was William Johns then commander of the privateer cutter *Sedwell*:

'Mr Job having desired me to certify to you that I am agreeable to pay your bills to him, in consequence of what hath been reported to you at Guernsey, I assure you that I am agreeable to pay the money to Mr Job and I shall pay him for your account in few days.
Polperro 4th December 1795
William Johns

In spite of the undertaking, Johns settled the debt by paying Lukis direct instead of giving the money to Job. To make matters worse, the *Sedwell*'s commander had attempted to enter into an arrangement with John Lukis through Charles Guy the landlord of the Ship Inn at Polperro, in place of Job. Such a threat to Job's virtual domination of the smuggling trade there was bitterly resented by him and he wrote indignantly to Lukis in May 1796 declaring:

'After the manner in which I have always behaved towards William Johns and his professions of friendship, both personally to myself as well as by his signature sent you, whereby he promised to pay me the money for your goods, all which he hath violated without assigning a single reason for so doing, it only remains for him to reconcile such conduct to his own feelings if he has any...
I hate deception. If he wished to remit your money he should have avowed it, and not signed his readiness to

pay it me - and continue to pretend he would pay it me when he knew he had remitted it, and all this under the mask of friendship. But there is no accounting for the conduct of some men nor for their ingratitude.'

While the incident had little impact on Job's dealings with the smugglers, it did signify the emergence of Charles Guy as a rival to his commercial interests with the Guernsey merchants. Guy had taken over the running of the Ship Inn from his father a couple of years earlier and relied on the smugglers to supply him with brandy, gin and rum. By 1798, he was dealing regularly with Carteret Priaulx & Co. That there was keen rivalry between him and Job is evident from Guy's correspondence with the St. Peter Port merchants:

'I hope your charge will not be more than Mr Maingy's as Mr Job is trying to do all he can to get Clements and Hutton to deal with the Messrs Maingys.'

Both Carteret Priaulx and the Maingys, with whom Job now dealt exclusively, were at this time being undercut by John Lukis who was also dealing with some of their customers in Polperro. One of the smugglers, Charles Hutton, had complained to Guy that he could get better terms from the Maingys, so he was promised lower prices on the next cargo he took from Carteret Priaulx.

Such competition inevitably had an effect on the price of the commodities sold at Guernsey. Sometimes Job found himself in dispute with the suppliers, as on one occasion when one of them supplied liquor in barrels that were found to be half a gallon smaller than those usually shipped!

Generally Job was on good terms with the Guernsey merchants, sending them gifts of mutton, poultry and game. They, in turn, would send him port wine and spirits and even provide occasional treats for the smugglers, as in 1800 when Nicholas Maingy and Brothers asked Job to spend £10.4s.6d on 'all your dealers, a treat at Christmas.' And in February 1802 the Maingy brothers were again debited the sum of

£9.18s.6d for a dinner for John Rowett and his ship's company at the New Inn on the quay at Polperro. From time to time, Job would write with a special request, as in May 1796 to Peter De Lisle & Sons:

> 'I'll thank you to send me a dollop of good Bohay tea and a quarter of best grey coffee for a particular friend.'

Rivalry between the Guernsey merchant houses might have been good for the smugglers but it only added to the difficulties and risks faced by Job for whom by far the most time-consuming business was extracting payment for the goods, a task that occupied far more time than he spent collecting orders.

From time to time the Guernsey merchants would come across from the island in person, calling on their agents such as Job and Charles Guy and chasing up outstanding debts. On one such visit in February 1795, Carteret Priaulx got caught in a severe snow storm near Plymouth from where he later wrote to his brother Thomas:

> 'I am uncommonly blind and unluckily the 13 miles walk in the snow has had so bad an effect on my sight that I am here a prisoner; [my eyes] are so inflamed I dare not stir... I am thank God a little better today and hope in the course of two or three days to go to Cawsand... For God's sake don't ship goods for Isaac Pearce nor [Charles] Bowden. I cannot conceive how you came to trust them. I shall think myself happy if I can receive the 195 pounds, but if I do it will not be without much trouble...'

Six years later, in April 1805, Carteret Priaulx was again in Cornwall checking accounts and collecting debts. Arriving in Polperro, he called on Charles Guy at the Ship Inn, only to find the family mourning the death of Guy's brother-in-law, William Rowett the previous night. 'Excess of drink has killed him,' he told his brothers in Guernsey.

The prospect that the British parliament might soon end smuggling from Guernsey did not seem to worry Carteret very much. 'I am glad we shall not be long troubled with this damn business,' he wrote, and later the same month while in Polperro, expressed hope that if just two or three more smuggling voyages could be made, they would reduce the firm's stock before the British anti-smuggling acts were applied for the first time to Guernsey and end the trade.

During the summer of 1805 the traffic of smuggled goods from Guernsey to Cornwall was at a low ebb, due in part to the vigilance of the Revenue cruisers patrolling the Channel during the long hours of daylight, but also because the threat of the new anti-smuggling laws deterred venturers. By the time the legislation came into effect that year, Job had virtually withdrawn from the trade with Guernsey that had brought such prosperity to so many in Polperro.

Only a few years earlier an incident occurred off the coast of Cornwall that was to have such far-reaching consequences for many of those involved that Job had already begun to sever his links with the smuggling trade and concentrate instead on his banking and other commercial activities.

12

The *Lottery* Incident

Occasionally, Job would speculate on the English State Lottery, both for himself and for his clients, including even Lady Trelawny. Since the price of a single Lottery ticket was around £16, it was usual to divide the cost into four or more equal shares. For the lucky few, prizes of as much as £20,000 awaited.*

The lottery came to have an altogether more ominous meaning for the inhabitants of Polperro after 1799 however, for it was also the name of one of the boats there that featured in the events that eventually led to Job relinquishing his role as the smugglers' banker. The episode began on a winter's night in 1798 with one tragic incident and was to end with another almost exactly two years later.

A fine single-masted cutter, the *Lottery* had come to the notice of Customs officials at Looe and Plymouth who suspected her of being engaged in the smuggling trade with Guernsey. The evening after Christmas in 1798 Ambrose Bowden, the chief Customs official stationed at Cawsand, a small fishing village below Rame Head at the entrance to Plymouth Sound, was alerted that a smuggling vessel believed to be the *Lottery* had been seen at anchor off Penlee Point about to unload a cargo of contraband.

Bowden wasted no time rounding up the four members

---

* The Cornwall Gazette in October 1801 advertised 60 tickets for the English State Lottery for sale at £16..2s each, offering four prizes of £20,000, four of £10,000, four of £5,000, five of £2,000, ten of £1,000 and 18,000 prizes of £18 each. Tickets were purchased from licensed Lottery offices.

of his boat crew and setting off in the dark to investigate. Working their way stealthily along the shore by the light of the moon, Bowden eventually saw the outline of a large vessel ahead. Drawing closer, he was able to see three smaller boats alongside her stern.

When they were about one hundred yards away, a voice aboard the cutter hailed the Customs boat:

'Ahoy there! What boat are you?'

'A King's boat,' Bowden called in reply.

At once there was commotion aboard the larger vessel and then another voice yelled:

'Keep off, you buggers, or I'll fire into you.'

Undaunted by the threat and displaying almost reckless courage, Bowden stood in the stern of the Customs boat clutching a blue Customs flag as his oarsmen pulled steadily closer. Unfurling the flag, he shouted back:

'This is a King's boat. A Revenue boat, and you can fire if you dare!'

Three shots suddenly rang out in quick succession, the flashes from their discharge puncturing the gloom around the stern of the cutter, followed by more shouts and noise aboard her. In the confusion, Bowden noticed that one of his bow oarsmen, Humphry Glinn had slumped forward letting go of his oar and called on him to keep rowing.

'He's been hit!' cried one of his companions, lifting him up.

Without hesitating, Bowden grabbed a loaded musket in the boat at his side and fired back in the general direction of the shots while the three remaining oarsmen pulled away to a safer distance. Reloading, Bowden continued firing at the cutter whose crew had already cut their cable and were frantically hoisting and making sail, firing astern as they did so. While the cutter gathered way before the wind, Bowden continued to fire at her until she disappeared in the dark, leaving the Customs boat to return to Cawsand Bay with the mortally wounded Glinn. There he was carried aboard a naval frigate, *HMS Stag*, whose surgeon certified that Glinn had died from a massive head wound, his skull shattered by a musket ball.

Aboard the *Lottery*, the crew made sail for Polperro, unaware that a Customs officer had been killed in the exchange of fire. Her commander, Richard Oliver, a tall, slim 27-year-old mariner and one of the vessel's several owners, had set out from Guernsey a few days earlier with the cargo of spirits and tobacco for Cawsand. From there it would have been taken on into Plymouth for consumption during the Christmas festivities.

When they arrived at Polperro the following morning, word of their encounter with the Customs boat at Cawsand quickly spread as they unloaded the remaining cargo. Only later that day did news of Glinn's death reach them. Aware that the killing of a Customs officer was a capital offence and that there would be an intensive search for those responsible, the *Lottery* crew quickly set sail again for Guernsey.

By the time Zephaniah Job came to read the account of Glinn's murder in the *Sherborne & Yeovil Mercury* in February 1799, many of the details were familiar to him from the gossip among those who lived at Polperro. Nevertheless, he would have been concerned by the official notice published by the Customs Commissioners, copies of which began to appear on posters in the area:

> 'His Majesty, for the better discovering and bringing to justice the persons concerned in this felony and murder, is hereby pleased to promise His Most Gracious Pardon to any one or more of the said offenders (except the Master or Commander of the said sloop or cutter, and

> the person or persons who actually fired) who shall discover his or their accomplices, so that any one or more of them may be apprehended.
> Custom House, London, January 22nd, 1799
> 'And as a further encouragement, the Commissioners of His Majesty's Customs, do hereby promise a Reward of Two Hundred Pounds to any Person or Persons (except as before stated) who shall discover and apprehend, or cause and procure to be discovered and apprehended, any one or more of the said offenders, to be paid by the Receiver General of His Majesty's Customs.
> By Order of the Commissioners, J.Hume.

Job knew very well that such a bounty would have been enough to tempt many people who might have information to give the authorities the lead they so eagerly wanted. For over five months those who had been aboard the *Lottery* on the fateful night off Cawsand kept out of sight of their pursuers, afraid even to sleep in their own homes in Polperro for fear of being taken by the dragoons who called there from time to time. Meanwhile, the *Lottery* itself continued to bring contraband goods across from Guernsey for Charles Guy the landlord of the Ship Inn, despite the hunt for her crew.

The *Lottery*'s luck finally ran out on the afternoon of Monday, May 13th that year when she was sighted off Start Point on the Devon coast by Gabriel Bray in command of the *Hind* Revenue cutter. Bray at once set off in pursuit, doggedly following the *Lottery* as she tacked close in and out along the shore in a desperate attempt to escape. After a chase that lasted through the night and into the following afternoon the two vessels were finally becalmed off Lands End where, after a brief skirmish, the *Lottery* and her crew of seventeen were seized as they abandoned the vessel and made for the shore. The following day they were brought into Plymouth along with the cargo of brandy, gin, tea and tobacco found aboard her at the time.

One of those taken aboard the *Hind* was a Polperro man named Roger Toms who had been on board the *Lottery* when

Humphry Glinn was killed. In order to gain a pardon for himself, Toms agreed to testify against those of his fellow crewmen who had been involved. He named another Polperro man, Thomas Potter, as having fired the fatal shot. As Potter was not among those captured by the *Hind*, Captain Bray wasted no time on arrival at Plymouth rounding up a party of dragoons and set off overland to Polperro. Arriving there by stealth at midnight, they were able to surprise Potter at home in bed and bring the startled man back to Plymouth where he was confined in the notorious 'Black Hole' dungeon in Devonport for three days before being formally charged with the murder of Glinn and taken eventually to Newgate gaol in London.

Two of the other prisoners captured by the *Hind*, William Searle and Thomas Ventin, were also named by Roger Toms as having been implicated in the murder of Glinn. The remaining *Lottery* crewmen were prosecuted and convicted for smuggling, five of whom were also charged with armed resistance and tried at the Old Bailey where they were sentenced to two years hard labour aboard the *Stanislas*, one of the leaking, rat-infested prison hulks moored on the Thames at Woolwich.

Toms, a key prosecution witness in the case against Potter, Searle and Ventin, was allowed to go free but, for his own safety, was made a member of the *Hind*'s crew. His freedom was short-lived, however. Just two weeks later, while the *Hind* lay at anchor in the Fowey estuary, Toms' wife Martha was persuaded to go to Polruan for a secret rendezvous with her husband.

As the couple walked together across the downs above Lantic Bay nearby, a group of Polperro men lying in wait seized Toms, carrying him off and shipping him across to Guernsey where he was held. Without him, the case against Tom Potter, Searle and Ventin could not proceed and the trial at the Old Bailey was postponed. Undeterred by the loss of their key witness, the authorities were still determined to prosecute the case against all the men

Polperro £5 banknote
(Royal Institution of Cornwall)

St Peter Port, Guernsey, in the early 19th century.
1831 sketch by Cecilia Markham (above)
and (below) the quay by Paul Jacob Naftel (1817-1891)
(Priaulx Library, Guernsey)

Polperro 23 Jany 1800

Messrs Carteret Priaulx & Co

Gentlemen

I have been duly favoured with your much
esteemed of the 8 inst and am happy to find the
May Flower continue to meet with some success —
I hope she will still be fortunate —

I have received and paid for your account,
since my letter to you of the 28 Ulto, as under —
Viz, Jany 2d   ⅌ Chas Hutton bill 7th Decr — 34 "
      3 — ⅌ Wm Minards & Co 22d Octr — 165 " "
           ⅌ Chas Hutton on acct of Goods } 50 "
              to be shipped ⅌ Betsey — }
      22 — ⅌ Wm Minards & Co — 22d Octr — 36 "
           ⅌ Philip Littleton — bill 10th Jany   16 .

Dr
Jany 3d To Anthony Priaulx, Nelsons } 200
             Dft on Esdaile —— }

P T O

Job letter to Messrs Carteret Priaulx & Co. (1800)
(Priaulx Library, Guernsey)

SHIP INN,

POLPERRO,

KEPT BY

CHARLES GUY.

Trewman and Haydon, Printers, Plymouth.

	£	s	d
Eating - - - -			
Wine - - - -			
Negus - - - -			
Rum - - - -			
Brandy - - - -			
Geneva - - - -			
Punch - - - -	0	1	3
Toddy - - - -			
Shrub - - - -			
Flip - - - -			
Beer - - - -			
Cyder - - - -	0	0	2
Cherry Brandy -			
Raspberry ditto -			
Coffee - - - -			
Tea - - - -	0	2	8
Firing - - - -			
Tobacco - - -	0	2	0
Lodging - - -			
Servants Eating -			
Drinking - - -			
Hay - - - -	0	2	8
Corn - - - -	0	2	0
Smith - - - -			
Ostler - - - -			
Chambermaid - -			
Waiter - - - -			
Boots - - - -			
Servants	0	10	9
	0	2	0
		12	9

Account for goods sold by Charles Guy
at the Ship Inn, Polperro, October 1790

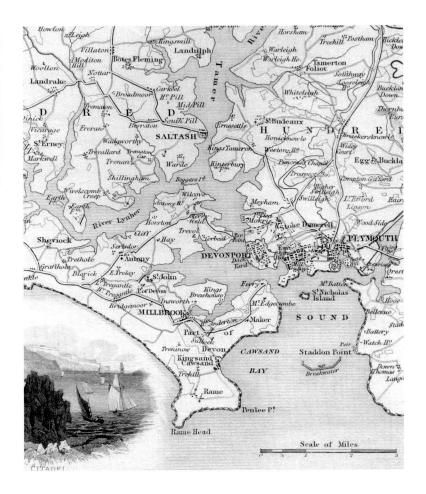

Map of Plymouth and district (1835)

WHEREAS it has been humbly represented to the King, that RICHARD OLIVER, the Younger, RICHARD BARRETT, the Younger, WILLIAM SWARTMAN, the Younger, PHILIP LIBBY, the Younger, THOMAS GEORGE, and ROGER TOMS, of Polperrow, in the county of Cornwall, mariners, and lately belonging to a smuggling vessel called the Lottery, stand charged upon oath with being concerned in the WILFUL MURDER of HUMPHRY GLINN, late a boatman belonging to the six-oared boat in the service of the Customs, stationed at Cawsand, on the 26th of December last, between the hours of ten and eleven at night, off Penlee Point, on the coast of Cornwall, by firing from on board the said vessel called the Lottery with muskets at the said boat.

His Majesty, for the better discovering and bringing to justice the above-named persons, is hereby pleased to promise his most gracious pardon to any one of the said offenders, (except Richard Oliver, the younger, the master of the said vessel, and Richard Barrett, the younger, one of the owners thereof, and the persons who actually fired) who shall discover his accomplice or accomplices, or be the means of any one or more of them being apprehended and committed to prison for the said offence.

PORTLAND.

And as a further encouragement, the Commissioners of his Majesty's Customs do hereby offer a Reward of Two Hundred Pounds to any one of the said offenders, (except as before excepted) or to any other person or persons who shall apprehend, or cause to be apprehended, any one or more of them, the said Richard Oliver, the younger, Richard Barrett, the younger, William Swartman, the younger, Philip Libby, the younger, Thomas George, and Roger Toms, whose descriptions are hereinafter mentioned ; which said reward will be paid by the Receiver-General of the Customs, upon the said persons, or either of them, being apprehended and committed to prison.

By order of the Commissioners,
J. HUME, Secretary.

Customs Commissioners Notice
Sherborne Mercury, 1799

The New Goal of NEWGATE.

Newgate Gaol (top)
A pirate hanged at Execution Dock
(The Malefactor's Register 1779)

Memorials to Polperro smugglers

Robert Mark's headstone in Talland Church (top)

John Perry, killed by a cannon ball in 1779,
Lansallos churchyard (below)

The names of six missing men and their descriptions were published, including that of Roger Toms described as having 'a very dark complexion, long face, balding with short curly black hair, about five feet six inches in height, of middling stature and has a rupture'. Although his age was given as 45 he was in fact only 41 years old. A reward of £200 was offered to anyone giving information leading to the arrest of any of the others named: Richard Oliver the *Lottery*'s commander, described as 'about 6 feet high, rather thin but very boney and walks very upright'; Richard Barrett, 'about 32 years of age, very thin and rather stoops in his walk'; Philip Libby, 'about 42 years of age, very stout'; William Swartman, 'about 24 years of age, long brown tied hair' and Thomas George, 'long thin face, very wide mouth, short black hair, rather bald, about 50 years of age and has lost part of the fore finger of one of his hands'.

Such detailed descriptions could only have been provided by Roger Toms who was eventually found the following year in Guernsey, having been identified by William Byfield in whose house in St. Peter Port he had been held. Returned to Plymouth aboard the Revenue cutter *Swift* in April 1800, Toms was taken at once under military escort to Exeter gaol where he was again interviewed by Gabriel Bray, intent on learning the whereabouts of the remaining members of the *Lottery* crew still at large, probably on Guernsey.

With their principal witness now safely returned, the authorities wasted little time bringing the case against Thomas Potter, William Searle and Thomas Ventin for the murder of Humphry Glinn at the Old Bailey early in June. Two other key prosecution witnesses, Ambrose Bowden, the Customs officer whose boat had intercepted the *Lottery* off Cawsand, and Hugh Pearce*, first officer of the *Hind* at the time the *Lottery* crew were taken prisoner, set off by coach together from Plymouth on June 4th to attend the trial in London. Bowden was taken ill at the outset, however, and by the time he had reached Exeter was feeling so unwell that he was unable to

---

* Hugh Pearce later became Superintendent of the Waterguard in the Channel Islands. He died in Polruan in 1825 at the age of 65.

travel on any further. He did eventually recover sufficiently to travel on as far as Egham in Surrey where, four days later, he lay so seriously ill at the Kings Head Inn that a local doctor certified that he could not possibly continue the journey to London 'without imminent danger to his life.'

In the face of such medical evidence and the absence of such an important witness, the prosecution had little option but to ask once again for the trial to be postponed until the Customs officer from Cawsand was well enough to attend and give evidence.

Was Bowden's mysterious and sudden illness genuine, or had he been got at? Back at Polperro, Zephaniah Job later secretly recorded a curious series of payments in connection with the *Lottery* trial, including one payment of £105 to Ambrose Bowden dated June 7th 1800, just two days before he was lying so dangerously ill at Egham. Perhaps Bowden had been bribed to swallow some toxic substance that induced the symptoms which prevented his appearance at the Old Bailey? Whatever the reason, it was certainly a very large sum of money to be giving one of the key prosecution witnesses in a murder trial involving the Polperro smugglers. Another item entered by Job records a further £112 on *'expence to and from London'* in June that year, no doubt in connection with the trial.

Whatever the reason for Bowden's indisposition, it did no more than delay the eventual trial for a further six months until December when, nearly two years after Glinn's murder, the three former *Lottery* crewmen appeared once more together in the dock at the Old Bailey.

The most damning evidence was given by Roger Toms who admitted being aboard the *Lottery* on the night in question and named the prisoners Potter, Searle and Ventin as well as those still sought in connection with Glinn's murder, including Richard Oliver, Richard Barrett, William Swartman, Philip Libby, Thomas George and a man known as Irish Jack as being on board at the time.

The main effort of the defence counsel was aimed at discrediting Toms and several witnesses were called to swear they knew him to be a liar and a thief. They, in turn, were closely cross-examined by the prosecuting counsel, intent on showing that they, as well as everyone else living near the coast, were smugglers and therefore interested in protecting the prisoners. The Admiralty judge, Sir William Scott, summed up by telling the jury of twelve men that everyone on board the *Lottery* at the time the shot that killed Humphry Glinn was fired was equally as guilty as the person who fired it. The question the jury had to decide was whether the prisoners were on board at the time, and that depended on the evidence of Roger Toms.

After retiring for nearly an hour, the jury returned a verdict of guilty against Thomas Potter for the murder of the Customs officer. Although William Searle and Thomas Ventin were acquitted of murder, they were nevertheless sentenced to the same two years hard labour on the Thames as the other members of the *Lottery*'s crew. The judge then pronounced the death sentence in the prescribed manner, addressing Potter at length and concluding with the macabre words:

'You will be conveyed to the place of execution on Friday next, and there hanged by the neck until you shall be dead, and your body afterwards given to be dissected and anatomised.'

Because of the unusually high tide on the Thames at the time, the wretched Potter was kept in one of the condemned cells at Newgate until the following week when, on Thursday December 18th, he was taken on the two mile journey by horse-drawn cart to Execution Dock at Wapping accompanied by the prison chaplain. There, at the turn of the tide, Tom Potter met his death at the age of 26 on the gallows set at low water mark by the customary method reserved for those convicted of crime on the high seas.* An Irishman from county Waterford, he

---

* Hangings at Execution Dock were conducted in a peculiar manner. The scaffold was placed so that the criminal's feet would reach to about the high-water mark and the body being suspended when the tide was low, was allowed to hang until the Thames rose and washed the feet of the corpse before it was cut down.

was attended by a Roman Catholic priest and, it was reported afterwards, conducted himself with great penitence.

The tragic outcome of the *Lottery*'s encounter with the Customs boat at Cawsand and the events that followed had far-reaching consequences for many of those involved. Despite efforts to conceal his involvement, it is now evident that Zephaniah Job went to considerable lengths to frustrate the prosecution of the case as well as do all he could to assist the unfortunate men captured by Captain Bray.

After the trial, Job made a pencilled note on a loose sheet of paper of the costs he had incurred under the heading '*Lottery*'. One item, dated May 15th 1799, the very day Tom Potter was seized at home in Polperro by Gabriel Bray and the dragoons, says simply: '*Gave Thos. Potter £1.1.0*', probably to enable him to buy his own food rather than survive on the prison swill. Another refers to the sum of sixteen guineas paid '*To the men in prison*', no doubt the 16 members of the *Lottery* crew confined at Plymouth. In all, Job spent more than £700 in various payments to lawyers in London and other expenses in connection with the trial, including the mysterious payment of £105 to Ambrose Bowden just before he was due to testify against Potter in June 1800.

Roger Toms had good reason to fear for his life if he ever returned to Polperro after Potter's execution. Even his family rejected him and he remained at Newgate gaol for the rest of his life employed as an assistant turnkey.

There was one other casualty of the *Lottery* episode. Humphry Glinn, already widower at the time of his murder, left a ten-year old son who had a serious speech impediment and was, according to the Plymouth Collector of Customs, 'destitute of friends and means of support'. The Customs Board in London agreed to pay for the boy to attend school at St. Germans in Cornwall until he became a tailor's apprentice.

Ambrose Bowden's courage in confronting the *Lottery* smugglers off Cawsand was rewarded with promotion to first officer aboard the Revenue cutter *Busy* at Plymouth in 1800.

For Gabriel Bray however, the capture of the *Lottery* was to be the ultimate success in his long campaign against the smugglers. Shortly after Potter's trial and execution, ill health compelled Bray to relinquish his command of the *Hind* after a career spanning nearly thirty years in the King's service at sea. Now aged 50, he continued to live at a house on the Esplanade at Fowey where he no doubt practiced the painting and drawing skills that had won him considerable acclaim as an artist in earlier years. Finally, in the summer of 1807 his property was sold by auction and he joined the roll of Greenwich naval pensioners, eventually retiring to Charmouth in Dorset where he died on October 23rd, 1823, at the age of 73.

13

The Revenue Men

In Polperro, the tragic outcome of the *Lottery* affair represented a kind of violent fin de siècle as the 18th century came to an end and another began. It is doubtful if those two adversaries, Zephaniah Job and Gabriel Bray, ever met face to face but for Job, now also turned 50 and troubled by the mounting losses suffered by the smugglers at the hands of the Revenue vessels, it was to be the turning point in his long involvement with a trade that had once brought great benefit to the community but now seemed only to bring distress.

While Tom Potter's widow, Mary, grieved for her husband, and the children of Roger Toms rejected their father, the hunt for the remaining members of the *Lottery* crew still at large continued. For months afterwards, the tranquillity of Polperro was broken by the dreaded sound of horses hooves in its narrow cobbled streets as detachments of cavalry came in search of them. Time after time the homes of the fugitives would be surrounded at the dead of night, but on each occasion they were spirited away with the help of friends and neighbours. Every movement of the conspicuous red-coats was watched as they marched through Polperro, muskets at the ready, searching everywhere for the missing men. No one talked; no one gave the men away despite the £200 reward, for fear that others might suffer the same fate as Tom Potter.

To make matters worse, the *Lottery* itself was taken into service by the Collector of Customs at Plymouth. Instead of suffering the usual fate of vessels seized for smuggling at that time, and ordered to be sawn into three pieces and the remnants sold at auction, she was soon back at sea under the command of Alexander Frazer employed in suppressing the very trade she had only recently been used for. In September 1799, only weeks after putting to sea, Frazer and his crew encountered two more Polperro vessels returning from Guernsey, the *Assistance* and the *Unity*. In the ensuing chase, the *Lottery* followed both all the way into Polperro harbour where the *Assistance* was boarded and found to be carrying 33 casks of contraband spirits. Despite the presence of three local Customs officers, the *Lottery's* commander had the utmost difficulty in seizing both the *Assistance* and her cargo before returning to Plymouth.

The Customs officers concerned, a Riding Officer named Nathaniel Prynn and two Boatmen, Charles Mallett and Samuel Sargent, were subsequently dismissed from the service for 'gross and criminal negligence in the execution of their duty' having withheld information and assistance from Frazer at the time.

The events of the previous months persuaded the Customs Board in London that further measures to combat smuggling at Polperro were necessary. They gave orders that a six-oared boat with a Sitter was to be stationed there and, accordingly, six men willing to serve as boatmen were selected from the crews of the Revenue cutters *Ranger* and *Busy*, Thomas Stap was appointed as Sitter and cutlasses, muskets, pistols and ammunition were issued to the crew. By April 1801, the first Customs boat was stationed at Polperro.

The arrival of what later became known as the Preventive boat caused considerable dismay among the smugglers who watched its arrival at the quayside. Such was the local hostility shown to the seven men that not a single household in Polperro would provide lodgings for them. Thomas Stap was compelled to ask his masters in Looe for a boat to be moored in the harbour for him and his crew to use as living quarters, and in due course a former smuggling vessel called the *Success* was sent round from Fowey for the purpose. The Preventive boat was required to pay a mooring fee like any other and Job, acting as steward for John Phillipps Carpenter who owned of the harbour, charged the Customs Collector at Looe an annual sum of six guineas.

At sea, the seizure of vessels engaged in smuggling by the Revenue cutters continued and in November 1801 a Customs official at Plymouth declared that smuggling 'has been much on the decline from the heavy losses the smugglers have experienced by captures made by the different cruisers and officers on this coast.'

The violent skirmishes between Customs and contrabandists that characterised the *Lottery* affair increased both on land and at sea. Even while the hunt for the *Lottery*'s crew was taking place in 1799, Christopher Childs, an Excise officer based at Looe was attacked by a gang of eight or nine smugglers at Pleaton between Polperro and Talland Bay. The *Sherborne Mercury* reported that the gang 'rescued from him two ankers of spirit liquors which had just been seized there, and also abused him and very much ill-treated him.' Despite the offer of a £20 reward for information leading to the conviction of the assailants, none was forthcoming.

When the presence of riding officers or coastguards made it too risky for contraband cargo to be landed, the smugglers would sink their kegs off-shore attached to a stout 'sinking rope' weighted with large stones to prevent them drifting. Well-secured in deep water, a cargo could lie for weeks without damage, though occasionally a fishing boat would land an unexpected catch. Job refers in a letter to one of the Guernsey merchants in 1797 to the misfortune of a Polperro smuggling vessel which, 'after getting clear of all the cutters in the Channel and sinking his cargo, it was all taken up by a trawl boat who refused to deliver it to them and carried it off, giving them only a few ankers.'

The Polperro smugglers suffered casualties of their own. At Talland church lies the headstone of Robert Mark one of the crew of the *Lottery* at the time it was seized by the Revenue cutter *Hind* in 1799. The *Cornwall Gazette* gave the following account in December 1801:

The Vulture smuggling lugger, brought into [Falmouth] by the Hind revenue cutter was in the act of sinking her goods (we understand) at the time the cutter fell in with her; and refusing to bring to, was fired into, when one man was killed and another wounded. The man who lost his life is said to be one who escaped the hulks on the Thames where he had been condemned for obstructing the officers of the Revenue.

Mark had evidently succeeded in escaping from the prison hulk *Stanislas* on the Thames at Woolwich where he had been serving the sentence of two years hard labour imposed the previous year in connection with the *Lottery* incident. The inscription on his headstone reads:

ROBERT MARK
late of Polperro, who Unfortunately
was shot at Sea the 24th day of Jany.
in the year of our Lord GOD
1802, in the 40th Year of His AGE

The epitaph at Talland is similar to one on a headstone still standing today in Lansallos churchyard recording the death of John Perry, killed by a cannon ball in 1779 at the age of 24. A couple of months after Robert Mark's unfortunate death, Job duly recorded in his ledger the payment of an outstanding debt by William Quiller on behalf of Mark from the Guernsey merchant, John Lukis:

Received of Mr Wm. Quiller from Mr John Lukis cash which
the late Robt. Mark borrowed in Guernsey £20..0..0

With the end of the War of the Revolution with France in 1802 came a brief respite during which time measures were introduced to curb the activities of the armed smuggling vessels that roamed the Channel.

A series of Government Acts intended to put a stop to the traffic in smuggled goods into Britain was approved by Parliament. Anyone found signalling from the shore to smugglers at sea was liable to a fine of £100, with rich rewards held out to informers. In 1805, an even more severe Act made it possible for any vessel found within 100 miles of the British coast with spirits, tobacco or tea in illegal packages on board liable to forfeiture. British anti-smuggling laws extended even to the Channel Islands, forbidding the movement of spirits, wine and tobacco to or from the islands in vessels of less than 100 tons. The powers given to Customs and Excise officers were also extended to naval officers, allowing them to impress any detained smuggler.

The Government introduced legislation allowing magistrates to sentence convicted smugglers to serve aboard a King's ship for a term of five years in the hope of making use of some of the experienced seaman found in smuggling craft. The harsh discipline that naval life was subject to at the time often encouraged pressed seamen to desert at the first opportunity.

The prospect of impressment into service aboard a naval man-of-war was feared more by the Polperro smugglers than imprisonment ashore. As early as 1787, Job had warned the Guernsey merchants that 'the men are fearful to go out to sea for the late bustle with Press-gangs.' And when Benjamin Rowett, who leased the New Inn* on the pier in Polperro from Job, had the misfortune to be impressed by a naval vessel while returning from the Channel Islands in August 1806, his wife Mary wrote to the Guernsey merchants, Carteret Priaulx asking for their help in obtaining her husband's release.

Rowett deserted while on shore duty in Portsmouth a few weeks later, but a 17-year-old Polperro youth named Robert Jeffery was not so fortunate when he was taken by HMS *Recruit* from a Polperro privateer in Falmouth harbour along with several other men in August 1807. The *Recruit* sailed for the West Indies where, in December of that year, Jeffery was marooned on the deserted Caribbean island of Sombrero

---

* Later the Pier Inn, leased by Richard Rowett in 1812. Although no longer an inn, the building still stands on the quay overlooking the inner harbour of Polperro.

without food or water for stealing the ship's beer. Although he was subsequently rescued by a passing American vessel, news of this callous act by the *Recruit's* captain, Warwick Lake, soon reached England where the case was heatedly debated in the House of Commons in 1810.

One of the MPs who took part in the debate, Samuel Whitbread, wrote to Zephaniah Job a few days later asking for information about Robert Jeffery.* Job readily replied, saying he had visited Jeffery's mother in Polperro:

'I found her in great distress on account of the cruel treatment her son had met with who she said she believed to be dead as she had never heard from him since the time he was so inhumanly put on shore on the island of Sombrero.'

Job related how he had also discovered that one of the other Polperro men impressed aboard the *Recruit* along with Jeffery, John Libby, had returned home. Libby described to Job how he had seen Jeffery put ashore on the island of Sombrero and was 'so shocked at the cruel treatment of his neighbour that he scarce knew what he did or what was done'.

'On their return to Barbados there was a report that Jeffery had been taken off the island by a frigate, whose name he could not recollect, and that he had eaten his flesh as far as his teeth could reach and died three days after his being on board.'

Job added a postscript saying he had also been informed that another young seaman from Polperro, Richard Oliver Johns, taken aboard the *Recruit* at the same time with his father, confirmed the grisly accounts of Jeffery flesh-eating and subsequent death.

---

* Samuel Whitbread, son of the London brewer, had been given Job's name by Dr. Oke Millett of Hayle, a relative of the Rev. John Millett, then curate at Lansallos.

A further letter from Job to Whitbread included a description of the missing youth, provided by his mother:

'He was 18 years of age the 11th of December 1807, two days before he was landed on the island; about five feet seven inches high and slight made at the time; oval face, rather a long visage, very light hair and eye brows. grey eyes, his left knee bent a little inwards.'

When Robert Jeffery eventually arrived home in Polperro in October 1810, he was given a hero's welcome. The celebrations, joined by everyone who lived there, surpassed even those that marked the end of the wars with France a few years later when Napoleon Bonaparte was brought into Plymouth on his way to St. Helena..

The end of the war against Bonaparte in 1815 immediately brought great changes, not least to the smuggling trade. The Government, anxious to reduce the cost of maintaining a large Navy at the end of a long and costly war, sought to deploy the considerable number of warships and sailors it had as quickly and as effectively as possible. There was concern that many of the thousands of seamen who were discharged would return to their old peace-time habits as free-traders, and one proposal was that the Revenue service should be reinforced in its battle against the smugglers.

Huge sums of revenue were still being lost as a result of the trade carried on by the smugglers and a number of new measures were introduced to counter it, including the introduction in 1817 of the 'Coast Blockade for the Prevention of Smuggling' along the Channel coast..

14

Spiritual and Temporal

Among the wealth of material relating to Zephaniah Job's life that remains today there is surprisingly little about the man himself. Few clues lie hidden among the pages of his mouldering letter-books, ledgers and papers to indicate just what kind of character he was and, since no portrait survives (if, indeed, one ever existed), his appearance can only be a matter for conjecture.

His early years in St. Agnes and the education he received in preparation for a career as a mine captain suggest he was not only an unusually bright scholar but was physically robust as well. Only once, in January 1796, does he ever refer to a bout of ill-health:

'I have been confined to my room for near a month last past with a violent cold which I took in my left shoulder and arm by too incautiously sitting against a current of air.'

Job remained a lifelong bachelor and there is no hint of any female relationships at any stage of his life. For the most part he lived alone in his cottage on Talland Hill* overlooking the harbour in Polperro, modestly in relation to his comparative wealth, and afforded himself little extravagance. What emerges from his copious correspondence is a portrait of a punctilious bachelor who would occasionally indulge himself as when ordering a new coat and waistcoat from his tailor in London in May 1975:

---

* Job's cottage on Talland Hill is believed to have been what is now Kayne Cottage.

'Let the cloth be of the best quality and the colour such as is now the most modest fashionable wear.'

More often, he would send word with one of the Polperro smuggling vessels to the Guernsey merchants for a shipment of port for himself, always adding 'please to order the best quality.' But he rarely, if ever, ventured across the Channel himself, although he did make a number of journeys by coach to London at different times of his life, usually in connection with privateering business and, on one or two occasions, to attend trials involving the smugglers. Lanes into and out of Polperro were too steep and muddy for the use of horse-drawn vehicles so Job always rode or walked locally.

His dealings with the smugglers and his involvement with incidents such as the seizure of the *Lottery* would certainly have come to the attention of the authorities. Indeed, long after his death local inhabitants insisted that on one occasion he was even arrested and imprisoned although there is no evidence of such among his surviving papers.

Sir Arthur Quiller Couch, grandson of Job's physician Dr Jonathan Couch, describes Zephaniah Job in one of his short stories as 'one of your sour, long-jawed sort, a bit of a lawyer, with a temper like Old Nick... a stickler for order; kept his accounts like the Bank of England, all in the best penmanship, with black and red ink, and signed his name at the end with a beautiful flourish, in the shape of a swan, all done with one stroke - he having been a schoolmaster in his youth, and highly respected at it until his unfortunate temper made him shy a child out of a window, which drove him out of business, as such things will.'

If that was an accurate description, Job seems to have mellowed in his later years when Sir Harry Trelawny's daughter Mary recorded in her diary: 'Mr Job is quite cheering, sees everything in bright colours.'

Despite his singularly biblical name, Zephaniah Job's involvement with the religious life of the community in which he lived seems to have been almost entirely secular. His stewardship for the Reverend Sir Harry Trelawny and other members of the clergy in the neighbourhood of Polperro was dictated by practical motives rather than any desire to be of more exalted service, and there are only very occasional references to his attendance at Lansallos church.

As well as acting for the Eastcott family after the death of the Reverend Richard Eastcott, the rector of Lansallos, in 1779, Job undertook to manage the affairs of his successor Benjamin Shipman. The parish church of Lansallos occupies a secluded position overlooking Lantivet Bay more than two miles to the west of Polperro. It was here that Shipman installed a curate, Thomas Donnithorne choosing to live elsewhere while relying on Job to collect his tithes from the parish and pay his outgoings. The arrangement continued with Shipman's successor, the Reverend Henry Pooley during whose term of office the parish was administered by the vicar of Talland.

Over a period of 30 years, Job collected more than £500 a year from the Lansallos parishioners on behalf of Pooley in tithes, the one tenth of the produce that an agricultural community was required to give each year towards the upkeep of the church and clergy. As well as pocketing the farmers' tithes, Pooley took good care to collect his tithes from the fishermen, though in some years when the fishermen were too busy smuggling to attend to fishing, the tithes were remarkably low. But most of the time the absentee cleric took his dues and gave little in return to the parish.

Sir Harry Trelawny on the other hand, as vicar of Egloshayle near Wadebridge for nearly a dozen years from 1793, did rather more for his parishioners if Job's accounts are any guide. He certainly took some personal interest in the place, visiting it from time to time and paying for the schooling of some of the children.

Sir Harry's extraordinary religious odyssey through life led him from Methodism in his youth at Oxford and ordination as a Presbyterian minister at the age of 21 until a change of heart led to him joining the Church of England in 1781, incurring the wrath of the sects he had successively patronised and then abandoned. He later offered refuge at Trelawne to two Catholic priests who had fled the French Revolution, one of whom taught Sir Harry's daughters, Anne and Mary, and eventually received them into the Catholic church. In due course, Sir Harry himself became a Catholic, having resigned as vicar of Egloshayle due to ill health and gone abroad to live in Germany where his great love of preaching continued to dominate his life. Only after the death of his wife in 1822 was his request for ordination as a Catholic priest granted by the Vatican.

During the early part of the nineteenth century, Sir Harry returned live at Trelawne and Job became a regular caller there, taking tea with the family, advising on business matters and generally treated as a friend and confidant.

Sir Harry himself was responsible for the founding of another remarkable religious institution near Polperro, Sclerder Abbey. He had given sanctuary at Trelawne to two Catholic émigré priests who had fled the terror of the French Revolution after 1793; an extraordinary gesture for a Protestant household at that time. The priests left Trelawne in 1802, but not before both of Sir Harry's daughters Anne Letitia and Mary had become Catholics. After their father's conversion to the Catholic religion and his eventual ordination as a Catholic priest in Rome in 1830, the Trelawny sisters established a Catholic church on a two-acre site above Polperro, about a mile south of Trelawne. The buildings were extended over the years and a number of religious communities, including Carmelite nuns, have lived there. Today the convent at Sclerder is still a centre of Roman Catholic worship.

Although Polperro is divided between the two parishes of Lansallos and Talland, Job had rather less to do with the ecclesiastical affairs of Talland where, sometime around 1812, a gentleman introducing himself as the Reverend Thomas Whitmore arrived and called on the vicar, Nicholas Kendall, offering his services as curate and letting it be known that he

ANNO QUADRAGESIMO QUINTO

GEORGII III. REGIS.

****

C A P. CXXI.

An Act for the more effectual Prevention of Smuggling.
[12th *July* 1805.]

WHEREAS in Defiance of the several Laws of Customs and Excise, great Quantities of Goods are illegally imported into, and landed in the United Kingdom, as well by clandestine Means as by open Force, to the great Detriment of the Revenue, and the Subversion of all Civil Authority: And whereas it is become highly necessary that some further Provision should be made for the Remedy of these great Evils: Be it therefore enacted by the King's most Excellent Majesty, by and with the Advice and Consent of the Lords Spiritual and Temporal, and Commons, in this present Parliament assembled, and by the Authority of the same, That, from and after the passing of this Act, if any Vessel or Boat coming from Foreign Parts, and belonging wholly or in Part to His Majesty's Subjects, or whereof One Half of the Persons on board shall be Subjects of His Majesty, (other than and except any Ship or other square-rigged Vessel), shall be found in any Part of the *British* or *Irish* Channels, or elsewhere on the High Seas, within One hundred Leagues of any Part of the Coasts of *Great Britain* or *Ireland,* or shall be discovered to have been within the said Limits, having on board any Foreign Brandy, Rum, Geneva, or other Spirits, in any Cask or Package of less Size or Content

Certain Vessels coming from Foreign Parts found in any Part of the British or Irish Channels, or High Seas, within a certain Distance of the Coasts of Great Britain or Ireland, having

16 Z

than

Robert Jeffery 1811
(National Portrait Gallery, London)

AN ACCOUNT OF THE SUFFERINGS OF

Jeffery the Seaman,

DURING HIS ABODE ON THE DESOLATE ROCK, OF

SOMBRERO

WHERE HE WAS LEFT

BY THE INHUMAN ORDER OF HIS CAPTAIN.

EXTRACTED FROM

A JOURNAL OR DAIRY,

DURING THE EIGHT DAYS HE REMAINED THERE.

With JEFFERY's Affidavit of his usage by the Captain,
And the particulars of the affectionate Meeting of Jeffery and
his Mother on his return to England.

Who is now to be seen at Mr. Wigley's Exibition room, Spring gardens.

Printed and Sold by J. Pitts, No. 14, Great St. Andrew-street
Seven Dials.

[PRICE ONE PENNY.]

J 45

1811 handbill advertising Robert Jeffery's story
(Essex Institute, Salem, Mass.)

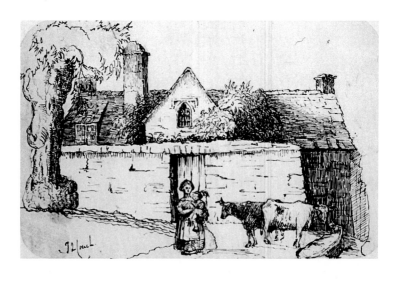

Sketch of Talland Vicarage by Thomas Quiller Couch

Talland Church interior 1904

Dr. Jonathan Couch (1789-1870)
(Royal Institution of Cornwall)

TO THE

Free & Independent Electors

OF THE

BOROUGH OF FOWEY.

GENTLEMEN,

At the Solicitation of many respectable Inhabitants of your Ancient and Independent Borough, we beg leave to offer ourselves as Candidates at the next **GENERAL ELECTION**, to represent you in Parliament. Should we be so fortunate as to become the objects of your Choice, you will ever find us ready to Support your Independence, and promote the general Interests and Welfare of your Port. In a short Time, we shall have the Pleasure of paying our respects to you in Person---until then,

We have the Honour to remain,

GENTLEMEN,

Your most obedient, faithful, humble Servants,

Valletort,

Alexander Glynn Campbell.

LONDON, 22nd MAY, 1818.

1818 General Election Handbill for Fowey MPs
Lord Valletort and Alexander Glynn Campbell

Name.	Abode.	When buried.	Age.	By whom the Ceremony was performed.
Zephaniah Job — No. 129.	Polperro in Talland	5th February	yrs 76	J. C. Millett Curate
Philippa Johns No. 130.	Polperro in Talland	16th February	78	J. C. Millett Curate
Joseph May No. 131.	Polperro	March	42	J. C. Millett Curate
Margaret Langmaid No. 132.	Trenewan	11th March	18	J. C. Millett Curate
Jane Puckey Fisher No. 133.	Polperro	17th March	Months 10	John C. Millett Curate
Ann Liddick No. 134.	Kellow	April 8	years 5	Wm Rawlings Minister
Mary Ann Fisher No. 135.	Polperro	April 14th	years 4	W Chartres Rector. —

Lansallos Burial Register (1822)

Polperro harbour viewed from Talland Hill. The initial work on the Duke of Cornwall pier on the east side of the harbour dates this photograph by Sir Harry Trelawny's grandson, Lewis Harding, as early as 1861.

The limekiln in the Warren, Polperro, once owned by Zephaniah Job.

(Photograph by Lewis Harding c1870)

had ample means. The stranger's offer was gladly accepted and he was soon settled in the vicarage at Talland, a secluded building surrounded by a high wall enclosing a courtyard so that only the upper half of the house, with its small Gothic windows and grey slated roof, was visible from the outside. There he entertained liberally, conducted church services with great solemnity and looked after the poor of the parish, earning the respect and affection of many. In due course, however, suspicion began to spread when his drafts at Job's bank in Polperro were dishonoured and it was not long before he was besieged by uneasy creditors demanding their money. The mysterious curate fled by night as suddenly as he had come, taking with him as much plate and other valuables from the vicarage he could carry.

Months later the 'Reverend' Whitmore was identified in Worcester as a well-known forger under the name of Robert Peacock where he was arrested, tried and convicted. A Polperro man passing through Gloucester in September 1814 witnessed the wretched felon's death on the gallows there, recognising him as the curate he had often heard preach at Talland church. When the news of the former curate's real identity reached Polperro, there was considerable consternation for he had officiated at many baptisms, marriage ceremonies and funerals during his time at Talland. Seven couples who had been married by the bogus curate came back to be married again, fearing their first ceremony had been invalid and they were 'living in sin'. The parents of eight babies baptised by the 'Rev. Mr Whitmore' between July and November 1812 brought them back to be baptised afresh.*

In earlier times, Talland church had been the source of ghost stories and tales of evil spirits. If there were spirits to be found in the churchyard, they were almost certainly of an altogether different kind for it would have been an easy matter

---

* The Talland parish register (now in the County Record Office at Truro) contains a note written by the vicar, Nicholas Kendall, explaining the double entries: "... it being suspected that Mr Whitmore, the late curate of this parish, was not a minister of the Church of England".

for smugglers to store kegs at such a lonely spot overlooking Talland Bay where they might have been brought ashore.

One vicar of Talland during the early 18th century, Richard Doidge, was an eccentric clergyman reputed to have great skills as an exorcist. One contemporary account describes how he would often be seen in the churchyard 'at dead of night to the terror of passers-by, driving about the evil spirits; many of them were seen, in all sorts of shapes, flying and running before him, and he pursuing them with his whip in a most daring manner.' The likelihood was that the 'shapes' were in reality local smugglers engaged in their nocturnal activities.

Perhaps more than anything else, John Wesley's two visits to Polperro in the 1760s ensured that the worst excesses of the trade engaged in by almost everyone there were avoided. The founder of Methodism preached there on both occasions, the last from the balcony of a house near the Green belonging to John Rommett. Rommett's home became the meeting-house for local Methodists until, in 1790, a small chapel was built nearby. Wesley frequently denounced smuggling as 'an accursed thing,' on one occasion threatening 'either they must put this abomination away or they would see my face no more.' In spite of this, Sir Harry Trelawny and some of Job's other clerical clients were content to accept occasional spiritual sustenance from the smugglers.

In the end, what probably did more to suppress smuggling in Cornwall than all the sermons preached by Wesley were the naval cutters employed after the Napoleonic wars, coupled perhaps with the effect that the popularity of drinking tea (one of the smuggled commodities) had on reducing the consumption of alcohol.

15

Death and Destruction

The golden age of the 'trade' as it was known in Polperro and elsewhere was already coming to an end when Sir Jonathan Phillipps, the owner of Raphael Manor whose steward Job had been for many years, died leaving an infant son to inherit the property to the west of Polperro. The trustees decided to sell the estate, and Job helped many of the Raphael tenants to buy their homes. Every property on the Raphael estate had been held on life leases of the tenants but for the first time in 700 years an Act of Parliament - the Phillipps Estate Act of 1813 - enabled anyone who could to buy the freehold.

Job himself paid £630 for 17 properties in Polperro, including the sand quay, the two lime kilns on the Warren, the slip where coal, goods and merchandise were landed and even the harbour itself:

'... all that the Haven or Harbour of Polperro extending from the sea at low water mark up the Beach to the Street called Lansallos Street as far as high water mark together also with the two Piers or Quay walls standing in the said harbour and the mooring rings and mooring places .... also all the Rock at the entrance of the said harbour called the Peak which is the sole defence of the said Harbour and Quay Walls in stormy weather .... and also a right is hereby given and granted to and for the said Zephaniah Job his heirs and assigns his workmen and labourers to dig search for and take stones wanting and sufficient for the reparation and rebuilding of the said Piers and Quay Walls from the path leading from Jane Mark's house by Chapel House to the Peak Rock.'

The harbour proved to be Job's one bad investment. In January 1817, just four years after he bought it, Polperro was hit by a storm of such terrible severity that it destroyed almost everything in the harbour.

The storm, when it struck, did so with even greater force and ferocity than so many others that had preceded it. Throughout the night the wind gathered strength, backing round to the south-east so that it confronted the incoming tide of water sweeping up the Channel from the Atlantic. By the time this wall of turbulent water had reached the southern shores of Cornwall in the early hours of Monday, the 20th of January, it threatened to overwhelm everything in its path. Fishermen heeded the warnings and those boats still at sea turned and headed for safety. Polperro, like dozens of other harbours along the coast, was the scene of frenzied activity as every available man and boy strove to secure the boats or haul them to safety. The shouts of the fishermen and screams of women and children above the noise of the wind gusting in from the sea in the early morning light echoed far up the narrow steep-sided creek.

With high water at dawn came huge waves that broke over the outer pier, flinging spray high into the air for the wind to carry across the flooded quay. Thick veils of cloud and driving rain enveloped the waterfront, sweeping in against the cottages that sheltered their occupants, and even the craggy outline of Peak Rock guarding the entrance to the harbour was fanged with foam. So great was the combined force of the elements that the storm drove the tidal flood up through the narrow coombe, surging over the Green and even stopping the mill wheel.

As the wind subsided and the tide receded men, women and children emerged from their homes to survey the damage, picking their way through the debris of seaweed, shingle and shattered timber that lay strewn across the quayside. Small boats had been hurled against the inner harbour wall, many dashed to pieces, others hanging precariously above the high water mark. Even the larger boats, moored as securely as their owners could make them, bore evidence of the strength and fury of the gale; broken spars, torn rigging, split timbers and paintwork chipped and scarred. For some, it would be many months before they could put to sea again.

The *West Briton* newspaper reported four days later:

'At Polperro the ruin is dreadful; out of 45 fishing boats belonging to the place 30 have been dashed to atoms; most of those remaining are incapable of being repaired. Upwards of 60 families are deprived of bread. The pier is nearly destroyed and several dwellings and cellars washed away. Two seans are totally lost and the greater part of the fish-salt in the town is washed away. Three new boats, all the timber and tools which were in the shipwright's yard have been carried away and the adjoining dwelling-house much injured. The loss to the proprietor, Mr John Rundle is nearly £800. The entire damage alone at Polperro is upwards of £6,000.'

For Job it was a devastating blow. He at once determined to have all the damage to the harbour repaired at enormous cost to himself. When Sir Harry Trelawny visited the scene in Polperro himself a few days later he was so moved by the plight of the fishermen who had lost their only means of livelihood that he immediately gave £30 for four new fishing boats to be built so that they should not starve. Even the Carpenter and Phillipps families who had previously owned the harbour contributed £100 towards the cost of repairing the quays. The sand quay was rebuilt at once and the shipwrights' yard a few weeks later. The rebuilding of the outer and inner piers lasted throughout the summer of 1817 and the outer pier was increased in height for greater protection against such storms. But for the inhabitants of Polperro who depended so much on the harbour and the boats that had been lost, it was a time of great hardship and distress.

The effort of repairing the damage left by the storm took its toll on Job. Although nearly 70 years old, his banking and commercial activities still demanded a great deal of his attention and, exhausted by the strain of rebuilding Polperro's shattered economy, his health began to suffer.

He was attended by Dr Jonathan Couch, the eminent Polperro physician and naturalist born there thirty years earlier. The only child of elderly parents who ensured he had a good education, Couch attended medical schools in London* before returning to settle in Polperro in 1810 where he applied his newly acquired surgical skills to the dissection and study of the marine life that was so vital to the welfare of his village. He made many drawings of the fish brought to him by the fishermen and these were later published in his major work, *The History of the Fishes of the British Isles*. This great work, containing 256 coloured drawings and water colours made by himself, is still recognised as being of considerable artistic merit as well as making a major contribution to scientific knowledge.

Jonathan Couch's first wife Jane died in childbirth and in 1815 the young doctor married Jane Quiller, one of the twin daughters of Richard Quiller, commander of the privateer *Lively* and son of Job's notorious smuggling and business associate, John Quiller.

For the last few years of his life Zephaniah Job lived in a cottage at Kellow near Crumplehorn Mill in the coombe above Polperro. During his final illness he was treated by Dr Couch until his death at the age of 73 on Thursday, the last day of January 1822. Job had dined heavily and heartily the previous evening, and was found dead in his bed in the morning.

Jonathan Couch would have paid one last visit to the home of his former patient and confidant to certify death. Five days later, Job's body was carried in its coffin by horse-drawn hearse along the lane that led to Lansallos church nearly three miles away, accompanied by the mourners on foot. There, after a simple service conducted by the Reverend John Millett, he was buried in the churchyard.

---

* There is an entry in one of Job's daybooks dated October 1808 for a cash payment of £10 to his London agent, Brock & Le Mesurier, for Jonathan Couch, then a student at the united medical schools of Guy's and St. Thomas' hospitals.

In due course, a headstone was erected over his grave with the following simple inscription carved by a local stone-mason, Robert Bishop:

> *In memory of Zephaniah Job, of Polperro*
> *merchant and banker, who departed this life*
> *the 31st day of January, A.D. 1822, in the*
> *75th year of his age.*

Curiously for a man who had always been so meticulous over the affairs of others, especially legatary matters, Job left no will of his own.

A thorough search of all his effects was made by William Minards who had been Job's clerk for two and a half years at the time of his death, but no will could be found. Cash amounting to £1,442 was counted up in Job's office in Polperro and this, together with bonds, bank notes and other cash due to him, was more than enough to honour all the promissory notes on his bank in circulation. The lease of the house, garden and orchard '*at Crenible Horn in Lansallos*' where he died, and his other properties were advertised for sale by auction in March 1822 along with livestock, barges and other shipping. Even his two horses ('they have been rode by Zephaniah Job Esq. and are well worth the attention of any gentleman or lady in want of a saddle horse') went under the hammer. After all expenses and other administration charges, including the sum of £135 for his funeral were deducted, his estate was valued at £7,766.

Letters of administration were granted to Zephaniah's two nephews Ananiah and Thomas Job and the proceeds of the estate was divided among the next of kin, though his elder brother John and sisters Elisabeth and Sarah were by then already dead.

After his death, many of Zephaniah Job's books, ledgers and papers were deliberately destroyed on a bonfire by certain people intent on making sure such documents did not fall into the hands of anyone else. On to the fire went the letter-books for the period between 1789 and 1795 when smuggling in Polperro was at its zenith, as well as those from 1798 covering the period of the *Lottery* incident. Just who it was that fed the flames and what they sought to conceal by such an act can only be guessed at. Job's habit of meticulously keeping a record of every letter and transaction would have been known to many who had good reason to want to prevent their affairs being known to others.

Rumours abounded for many months, speculating on the great fortune he was supposed to have left. Many believed he had always intended to make Sir Harry Trelawny his heir, others that he had at one time planned for his young nephew and namesake, Zephaniah, who he had employed as a clerk nearly thirty years earlier, to inherit the business. Whatever plans he may have had for his considerable wealth and business interests, intestacy must have been the least likely for a man who had spent so much time painstakingly drawing up wills for other people.

For nearly half a century, Zephaniah Job had contributed to the welfare and prosperity of the community in which he had once sought refuge. He brought with him knowledge and learning that he passed on to a generation of Polperro children before using his talents to develop the trade that had been carried on there long before his arrival. He served rich and poor alike, helping those in distress, lending money to those in need and furthering the aims of those who were willing to risk all on a venture. The wealth that he generated left a legacy far more durable than any other he may have planned in the event of his death, for it gave rise to a better-educated and more enterprising community than he encountered when he first arrived there.

Ananiah Job who had inherited a twelfth part of his uncle's estate amounting to £647, came to live in Polperro with his second wife, Elizabeth, whom he married in St. Agnes nine years earlier. By the time of his death in 1829 at the age of 54, he had made arrangements for Elizabeth and their six surviving children to be provided for. Elizabeth was to remain in the house in Polperro which they had occupied for as long as she continued to live there. She was also to have an annuity of £18, chargeable on the rents for a limekiln and garden in East Looe and another limekiln and house in Polperro called Will's House.

Ananiah's will had been drawn up by Jonathan Couch who made a curious, though perhaps pardonable, error in doing so, for it begins with the words: *I, Zephaniah Job of Polperro.....* Couch later had to make a sworn statement that 'Zephaniah' was a mistake for 'Ananiah'. The Couch family were then still close friends with the Job family in Polperro, and the will was witnessed by Jonathan's son, Richard Quiller Couch, the father of Sir Arthur Quiller Couch.

Jonathan Couch lived until 1870 when he too died peacefully in bed at his home in Polperro at the age of 82. Among his papers was the handwritten manuscript of his *History of Polperro*, published the following year. In it, he wrote of Zephaniah Job, whom he described as 'a man of singular sagacity and energy':

> "He became the accountant of most of the smuggling companies of Polperro, and the agent for receiving the sums due to the merchants of Guernsey; and it is a proof of his prudence that though acting for smugglers at a time when the business was a very successful one, he never joined them, and had no share in the risks or profits of privateering. He turned his attention to general business, and was prosperous in it. He continued to amass money, and lived in very respectable style until his death, when he left a good fortune to his administrators.'

It was a fitting, if not wholly accurate, tribute by one prominent Polperro figure of another, for not even Jonathan Couch had the advantage of access to the records and papers of Zephaniah Job so providentially preserved for posterity.

In all probability, the debt owed by generations of Polperro families to the remarkable 'Smugglers' Banker' is greater even than present day inhabitants of the Cornish fishing port will ever know.

APPENDIX

SEIZURES OF POLPERRO BOATS BY REVENUE VESSELS
(1791-1804)

Year	Seized By	Owner(s)	Boat
1791			
Nov	*Sprightly*	William & Richard Rowett Jr	
	Hind (Capt. Bray)	John Batten; Richard Mutton	
	Hind	Richard Oliver	
	Resolution	Richard Oliver	
	Greyhound (Capt. Weston)	Richard Rowett Jr & Co.	
Dec	*Resolution*	William Langmaid	
	Hind	Francis Johns	
1792			
Feb	*Spider*	Reginald Barrett	
	Resolution	Richard Barrett Sen	
Mar	*Sprightly*	John Toms	
	Spider	Charles Bowden	
Oct	*Hind*	William Rowett	
Nov	*Ranger*	Richard Oliver	
	Hind & *Spider*	William Johns Jr	
1793			
	Resolution (Lt Prideaux)		
	& *Hind*		*Assistance*
1794			
July	*Eagle*	William Johns & Co.	
1795			
Mar	*Eagle*	John Toms	
May	*Greyhound*	Robert & John Mark	
May	*Spider*	John Clemence & Co.	
May	[?]	Richard Rowett	*Happy Return*

SEIZURES OF POLPERRO BOATS BY REVENUE VESSELS
(1791-1804)

Year	Seized By	Owner(s)	Boat
1796			
July	*Hind* (Capt. Bray)		
Sep	*Pilot*	William Johns	
1797			
June	*Constitution* (Lt. Weston)	John Quiller	*Vigilant*
1798			
Jan	*Vigilent*		*Mayflower*
Feb	*Constitution*		*Venus*
1799			
May	*Hind*	Richard Oliver	*Lottery*
Sep	*Lottery*		*Assistance*
1800			
June	*Spider*		*Expectation*
1801			
Feb	*Ranger* (Lt. Frazer)		*Providence*
	Ranger (Lt. Frazer)		*Mayflower*
1803			
Feb	*Ranger*		*Patience*
1804			
May	*Humber*		*Brilliant*

ZEPHANIAH JOB ACCOUNTS: 1787 1805 [ZJ16 RIC]

1.   The Rev. Sir Harry Trelawny, Bart.
2.   The Executors of the late Susanna Eastcott of Lostwithiel
3.   Miss Ann Eastcott of Lostwithiel
4.   Miss Susanna Eastcott of Lostwithiel
5.   The Rev. Mr Shipman of St Teath
6.   Messrs John Grigg & Co.
7.   Messrs De Jersey & Corbin of Guernsey
8.   Messrs Jersey & De Lisle of Guernsey
9.   Messrs De Carteret & Co. of Guernsey
10.   Messrs Nicholas Maingy & Sons of Guernsey
11.   Messrs Perchard & Brock of London
12.   Messrs William Pinwill and Joseph Moore of Plymouth
13.   The Owners of the Sloop Three Brothers
14.   The Owners of Herierdsfoot Mine, Capt. Martine
15.   The Rev. Mr Bedford, Vicar of Talland
16.   Mr John Baker of Polperro
17.   The Rev. Mr Cory
18.   Mr John Lukis of Guernsey
19.   Mr John Quiller of Polperro
20.   Mr Robert Grigg of Looe
21.   Mr Carteret Priaulx & Co. of Guernsey
22.   Mr Richard Quiller of Polperro
23.   Messrs John Quiller & Sons of Polperro
24.   Mr William Johns of Polperro
25.   The Rev. Nicholas Dyer of Venn in Devon
26.   Sir Jonathan Phillipps Kt. & John Phillipps Carpenter Esq.
27.   Thomas Sandford Eastcott of Port Looe Esq.
28.   Mr John Owen Parr of London
29.   Messrs Perchard Brock & Lemesurier of London
30.   Messrs Job & Grigg
31.   Richard Carpenter Esq of Ireland
32.   Messrs F.Commerell Lubbock & Co. of London
33.   Messrs Porter & Huddart of Leghorn in Italy
34.   Messrs Stickling & Co. of Leghorn
35.   Messrs B.Nicholas & Co. of Naples
36.   The Rev. and Mrs Pooley of Truro
37.   Messrs Smith St. Barbe & Marten of London
38.   Mr John Robilliard of Alderney
39.   Mr John Mitchell of Guernsey
40.   Messrs Hillary Boucaut & Co. of Guernsey

ZEPHANIAH JOB ACCOUNTS: 1801 1816 [ZJ40 RIC]

1802	John James Esq.
1802	Messrs Taylors & Bollmain ...
1803	Messrs James Greenwood & Co. of London
1810	Mr William Wills of Plymouth Dock
1803	Brock & Mesurier of London
1803	Messrs Wilson Thomas & Co. of Truro
1803	Mr James Wynn of Falmouth
1803	Messrs Euke & Hutchens, London
1804	Joseph Banfield of Falmouth
1804	Messrs Thoume Moullin & Co. of Guernsey
1804	Messrs Chapple & Kneebone of Truro
1804	J.P.Carpenter Esq. & Thomas Phillipps Esq
1804	Mr Nicholas Robilliard of Weymouth
1804	Mr William Harrison
1804	Revd. Richard Cory of St Keynes
1804	Mrs Maria Robinson of Salisbury
1806	Mr Philip Brown of London
1806	Messrs Hillary Boucaut of Guernsey
1805	Mr Thomas Hoskins of Gosport
1806	Messrs Bovell & Hanbury of London
1806	Messrs Brock Lasere Maingy & Co.
1806	Messrs Langmaid of Plymouth
1806	Mr Stephen Fitchett of Fareham
1806	Sir Harry Trelawny
1806	John Lukis
1807	John Cooke Harding Trelawny Esq.
1808	Lieut. Thomas W. Nicholls
1813	Mr Richard Nicholls
1808	Messrs Bush & Were of London
1808	Mr Thomas Hugo of Lostwithiel
1808	Mr Joseph Cave of Portsmouth
1808	Mr Thomas Cornish Miller St. Germans
1809	Mr Philip Browne of London
1810	Mr John Fowler of Polperro
1810	Revd. Henry Pooley
	The Bishop of Exeter
1811	Christopher Smith Son & Co. London

Zephanias JOB
b 1705 St. Agnes   *d* 1769
m **Sarah**

Zephanias
bp 29/9/1735
St. Agnes

John
bp 25/1/1737
St. Agnes
m **Mary Williams**
13/2/1773 St. Agnes

Elisabeth
bp 4/10/1740
St. Agnes
m **Jonah Tonkin**
22/5/1763 St. Agnes

Sarah
bp 30/11/1744
St. Agnes
m **Francis Harris**

ZEPHANIAH
bp 22/1/1750
St. Agnes
d 31/1/1822
Polperro

Zephaniah
and John
bp 2/11/1773

Ananiah
bp 1/4/1775
St. Agnes
m(1) **Jane Solloman**
13/12/1794 St. Agnes

m(2) **Elizabeth Stephens**

Thomas
bp & *d* 1777
St. Agnes

Thomas
bp 14/2/1779
St. Agnes

Joseph Williams
bp 21/1/1781
St. Agnes

Mary Williams
bp 21/7/1782
St. Agnes
m **Joseph Rowett**
4/10/1830 Talland

Elizabeth
bp 25/5/1795
St. Agnes

Zephaniah
bp 22/1/1798
St. Agnes

John
bp 23/9/1798
St. Agnes

William
Solloman
bp 23/7/1800
St. Agnes

Jane
bp 14/11/1802
St. Agnes

Ananiah
bp 7/9/1806
St. Agnes
m **Maria Johns**
14/10/1830
Talland

Mary
bp 4/9/1809
St. Agnes

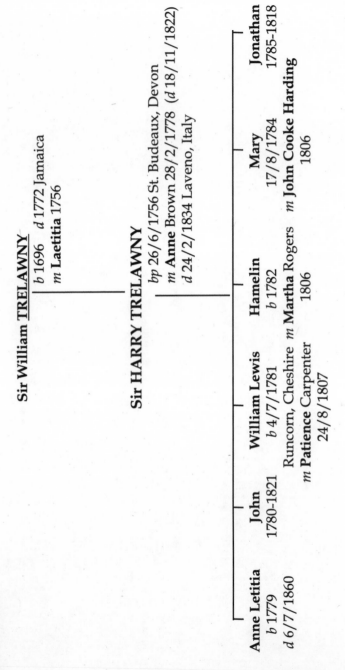

Sir William **TRELAWNY**
b 1696   *d* 1772 Jamaica
m **Laetitia** 1756

Sir **HARRY TRELAWNY**
bp 26/6/1756 St. Budeaux, Devon
m **Anne** Brown 28/2/1778 (*d* 18/11/1822)
d 24/2/1834 Laveno, Italy

Anne Letitia
b 1779
d 6/7/1860

John
1780-1821

William Lewis
b 4/7/1781
Runcorn, Cheshire *m* **Martha** Rogers
m **Patience** Carpenter   1806
24/8/1807

Hamelin
b 1782

Mary
17/8/1784
m **John Cooke Harding**
1806

Jonathan
1785-1818

SOURCE REFERENCES

1. Fugitive From St. Agnes

P.12 L.11 St. Agnes Baptisms FP2/1/2; Cornwall CRO.

P.13 L.8 M.H.Bizley, *Friendly Retreat* (1955) pp. 113-115.

P.13 L.31 Jonathan Couch, *History of Polperro* (1871) p.89.

P.14 L.5 George Henwood, *Cornwall's Mines and Miners* (1972) pp. 43-44.

P.15 L.6 Couch, *op.cit.* p.89.

2. Polperro Schoolmaster

P.17 L.4 John Wesley, *Journal* Vol.IV p.527.

P.18 L.19 John Clements' Exercise Book; ZJ6 Royal Institute of Cornwall.

P.21 L.24 John Rowe, *Cornwall in the Age of the Industrial Revolution* (1993) p.276.

P.22 L.22 Rowe, *op. cit.* p.274.

3. Freetraders and Privateers

P.23 L.12 Letter-book of Jean Guille & Co., Priaulx Library, Guernsey.

P.24 L.7 Zephaniah Job Day-book (1778-1787); ZJ7

P.26 L.7 HCA26/55/, Public Record Office.

P.26 L.24 ZJ7.

P.27 L.5 Customs Board to Plymouth Collector, 26 May 1794. CUST66/76, PRO.

P.27 L.17 Job Letter-book, 26 September 1797, ZJ32 RIC.

P.28 L.7 CUST66/75.

P.28 L.13 *Ibid.*

P.28 L.33 Henry Shore, *Smuggling Days and Smuggling Ways* (1892), p.219.

4. The Swallow's Tale

P.30 L.15 HCA32/444, PRO

P.31 L.34 HCA32/458, PRO

P.32 L.37 Job Letter-book 20 February, 1787, ZJ11a RIC.

P.33	L.12	*Ibid.* 15 August 1788.
P.33	L.18	HCA32/291, PRO.
P.33	L.22	HCA32/445, PRO.
P.33	L.26	HCA32/449, PRO.
P.34	L.3	Frank. H. Perrycoste, *Gleanings from the Records of Zephaniah Job of Polperro* (1930) p.147
P.34	L.13	ADM43/29, PRO.
P.35	L.6	ADM1/2307, PRO.
P.35	L.18	*Ibid.*
P.36	L.5	ZJ7.

5. Trelawny Steward

P.37	L.14	8 January 1786, ZJ11a.
P.38	L.1	Carole Vivian, *The Trelawnys* (1990) p.17.
P.38	L.9	Mrs A.E.Bray, *Trelawny of Trelawne* (1837) p.12.
P.39	L.6	19 August 1786, ZJ11a
P.39	L.14	*Ibid.* 28 August 1786.
P.39	L.19	*Ibid.* 25 August 1786.
P.40	L.1	*Ibid.* 30 April 1787.
P.41	L.1	*Ibid.* 16 September 1786

P.41	L.8	*Ibid.*
P.41	L.19	*Ibid.* 4 November 1788
P.42	L.10	*Ibid.* 28 February 1787.
P.42	L.20	Perrycoste, *op.cit.,* p.35.
P.44	L.1	5 October 1795, ZJ32.
P.44	L.31	Job Ledger (1787-1805), ZJ16 RIC.
P.45	L.24	Perrycoste, *op.cit.,* pp.28-29.
P.46	L.10	*Ibid.* p.118.
P.46	L.24	Mary Harding Diary, 21 May 1816, RIC.
P.47	L.1	*Ibid.* 1 April 1815.
P.47	L.15	*Ibid.*
P.47	L.23	ZJ21.
P.47	L.28	*Ibid.*

6. The Tragic Quillers

P.50	L.12	September 1786 ZJ11a.
P.51	L.2	Perrycoste, *op.cit.,* pp.148-149.
P.51	L.14	18 May 1795, ZJ32.
P.52	L.1	Couch, *op. cit.,* p.9.
P.52	L.11	31 May 1785, ZJ11a.
P.53	L.9	Job Ledger (1799-1805), ZJ35 RIC.
P.54	L.1	27 June 1797, ZJ32.
P.54	L.16	*Ibid* 22 Nov1797

7. Captain Gabriel Bray

P.55	L.18	Customs Board to Plymouth Collector, 5 Aug 1791. CUST66/75 PRO.
P.56	L.11	R.J.Cootes, *Britain since 1700* (1982) p. 152.
P.56	L.18	Old Bailey Sessions papers, Vol.72 pt.II, p.1325.
P.58	L.13	November 1795, ZJ32.
P.58	L.27	*Ibid.* 10 March 1796.
P.59	L.5	*Ibid.*
P.59	L.12	*Ibid.* 15 July 1796.
P.59	L.32	ADM7/328 PRO.
P.60	L.1	CUST31/3 PRO.
P.61	L.35	1 August 1797, ZJ32.
P.62	L.3	*Ibid.* 14 September 1797.
P.62	L.7	KB32/2, PRO.
P.63	L.23	KB11/60, PRO.

8. Revolutionary War

P.64	L.16	ZJ16.
P.64	L.22	HCA32/687/21 PRO
P.65	L.3	Perrycoste *op. cit.*, p.154.
P.65	L.3	December 1796, ZJ32.
P.66	L.7	ADM7/328.
P.66	L.8	CUST31/4 PRO.
P.66	L.25	26 January 1798, ZJ32.
P.67	L.4	Cyril Noall, *Old Cornwall* Vol.VI No.3 pp. 109-113.
P.67	L.20	*Cornwall Gazette*, 24 October 1801.
P.68	L.11	HCA26/88 PRO.
P.68	L.23	*Ibid.*
P.69	L.23	Mary Harding Diary, 27 June 1815.

9. Man of Business

P.70	L.25	Perrycoste *op.cit.*, pp.160-161.
P.71	L.9	*Ibid.*
P.71	L.23	*Ibid.* p.12.
P.72	L.2	Job Letter-book 8 December 1818, ZJ50 RIC.
P.72	L.12	Ibid. 23 December 1818.
P.72	L.29	*Ibid.* May 1819.
P.73	L.19	22 August 1795, ZJ32.
P.73	L.28	Perrycoste *op. cit.*, pp.129-130.
P.73	L.32	19 January 1796, ZJ32.
P.74	L.32	*Ibid.* 12 March 1797.
P.75	L.17	Perrycoste *op. cit.*, p.161.
P.75	L.26	Mar 1796 ZJ32.

| P.76 | L.8 | Job Ledger (1801-1816) ZJ40 RIC. |
| P.76 | L.15 | 29 May 1819 ZJ50. |

10. Smugglers' Banker

P.77	L.10	ZJ16.
P.77	L.17	Perrycoste *op. cit.*, p.32.
P.78	L.13	ZJ16.
P.78	L.30	*Ibid.*
P.80	L.1	31 October ZJ32
P.80	L.28	*Ibid.* 13 Sept 1797.
P.81	L.19	20 January 1788, ZJ11a.
P.81	L.37	*Ibid.* 6 Sept 1788.
P.82	L.4	*Ibid.* 20 January 1788.
P.82	L.18	ZJ39.
P.82	L.32	ZJ40.
P.83	L.8	1 March 1819, ZJ50.
P.83	L.22	*Ibid.* 29 April 1819.

11. Guernsey Merchants

| P.84 | L.13 | Canon Peter Raban, *Clandestine Trade in the Mid-Eighteenth Century* (1987) p.132. |
| P.85 | L.2 | Peter Johnston, *A Short History of Guernsey* (1987) p.56. |

P.85	L.27	Perrycoste, *op. cit.*, p.133.
P.86	L.5	11 November 1786, ZJ11a.
P.86	L.8	*Ibid.* 23 Sept 1788.
P.86.	L.20	*Ibid.* 17 January 1789.
P.86	L.31	7 June 1795, ZJ32.
P.87	L.13	*Ibid.* 26 June 1795.
P.87	L.23	*Ibid.* 10 May 1796.
P.88	L.1	*Ibid.* 5 Dec 1795.
P.88	L.12	*Ibid.*
P.88	L.27	*Ibid.* 24 May 1796.
P.89	L.8	James P. Derriman, *Killigarth* (1994) p.122
P.89	L.14	Carteret Priaulx Papers,1 Feb 1798. Priaulx Library, Guernsey.
P.89	L.33	ZJ34.
P.90	L.5	24 May 1796, ZJ32.
P.90	L.19	13 February 1795, CPP.
P.90	L.33	*Ibid.* 22 April 1805.
P.91	L.3	A..G. Jamieson, *A People of the Sea* (1986) P.214

12. The Lottery Incident

| P.92 | L.15 | HCA1/25/341, PRO. |

P.95	L.22	19 April 1799, CPP.
P.95	L.24	HCA1/25.
P.96	L.3	18 May 1799, CUST66/1, PRO.
P.96	L.20	HCA1/85/282, PRO.
P.97	L.1	*Sherborne Mercury*, 4 November 1799
P.97	L.19	2 May 1800, CUST 66.
P.98	L.5	HCA1/25/359, PRO.
P.98	L.14	J.R..Johns, *Polperro's Smuggling Story* (1994)p.60
P.98	L.28	HCA1/85/193, PRO
P.99	L.20	HCA/25/341, PRO.
P.99	L.22	HCA1/85/244 PRO
P.100	L.10	Johns *op. cit.*, p.62.
P.100	L.27	18 May 1799, CUST66/1.
P.101	L.7	*Johns op. cit.*, p.63.
P.101	L.11	*Cornwall Gazette*, 13 June 1807.
P.101	L13	*Mariner's Mirror*, Vol. 81, No.1 p.32.

13. The Revenue Men

| P.102 | L.24 | 29 June 1799, CUST66/1. |

P.103	L.1	*Ibid.* 23 September 1799
P.103	L.11	*Ibid.* 3 January 1801.
P.103	L.20	Customs Board to Looe Collector, 27 Jan 1801 CUST31/7.
P.103.	L.31	*Ibid.* 5 May 1801.
P.103	L.36	ZJ40.
P.104	L.4	CUST66/2.
P.104	L.15	*Sherborne Mercury*, 7 October 1799.
P.104	L.27	1 August 1797, ZJ32.
P.105	L.25	ZJ34.
P.106	L.19	1 November 1787, ZJ11a.
P.106	L.26	Carteret Priaulx Papers.
P.106	L.31	J.P.Derriman, *Marooned* (1991), p.11.
P.107	L.10	15 April 1810, Whitbread Papers 5238, Beds RO.
P.108	L.1	*Ibid.* 21 April 1810, 5243.

14. Spiritual and Temporal

P.109	L.13	22 January 1796, ZJ32.
P.110	L.1	*Ibid.* 20 May 1795.
P.110	L.20	Sir Arthur Quiller Couch, *The Capture of the Burgomeister*

		Van Der Werf (1927).
P.111	L.18	Perrycoste, *op. cit.,*pp.85-90
P.112	L.19	J.P.Derriman, *Sclerder And The Trelawnys,* South Western Catholic History (1986).
P.113	L.15	J.P.Derriman, *Western Morning News* 14 September 1984.
P.114	L.5	Charles G. Harper, *The Smugglers* (1909) p.184.
P.114	L.20	F.E.Halliday, *A History of Cornwall* (1959) p.272.

15. Death and Destruction

P.115	L.7	Sheila de Burlet *Portrait of Polperro* (1977) p.22.
P.115	L.11	*Ibid.*
P.116	L.30	*Ibid.* p.12.
P.117	L.22	Mary Harding Diary, 27 Jan 1817.
P.118	L.20	Perrycoste, *op. cit.,* p.162.
P.119	L.4	Couch, *op. cit.,* p.53.
P.119	L.13	Perrycoste, *op. cit.,* pp.163-164.
P.119	L.26	ZJ52, RIC.
P.119	L.33	Perrycoste, *op. cit.,* p.1.
P.121	L.7	Ananiah Job Will dated 26 September 1829, CRO.
P.121	L.21	Couch, op. cit. p.90.

INDEX